Understanding Giftings, Callings & Appointments

Let's Get It Right!

Rethinking How We Look at the Body of Christ

BY

Dr. Ron Horner

Understanding Giftings, Callings & Appointments

Let's Get It Right!

Rethinking How We Look at the Body of Christ

by

Dr. Ron Horner

LifeSpring Publishing
PO Box 2167
Albemarle, North Carolina 28002
USA

Let's Get it Right! by Dr. Ron Horner

Copyright ©2018

Scripture is taken from the New King James Version.® Copyright ©1982 by Thomas Nelson. Used by permission. All rights reserved.

AENT signifies Scripture taken from the Aramaic English New Testament. Copyright ©2008 Used by permission of Netzari Press.

All rights reserved. This book is protected by the copyright laws of the United States of America. This book may not be copied or reprinted for commercial gain or profit. The use of short quotations or occasional page copying for personal or group study is permitted and encouraged. Permission will be granted upon request.

Requests for bulk sales discounts, editorial permissions, or other information should be addressed to:

LifeSpring Books
PO Box 2167
Albemarle, NC 28002 USA

Additional copies available at www.lifespringbooks.com

ISBN: 978-1-387-77417-3 TP

eBook: 978-1-387-77421-0

Cover Design by Darian Horner Design (www.darianhorner.com)

Cover Image: Adobe Stock #72979172

First Printing: May 2018

Printed in the United States of America

10 9 8 7 6 5 4 3 2 1

Table of Contents

Acknowledgement.. I

Preface.. III

Introduction A Fresh Look at 1 Corinthians 12 1

An Overview.. 6

Contemporary Examples.. 8

Analyzing the Passage.. 11

Corresponding Grace.. 12

SECTION 1... 17

   Motivational Gifts & The Individual Believer................... 17

   Prophetic Perceiver 21

   Server 26

   Teacher.. 29

   Exhorter 32

   Giver.. 35

   Ruler/Leader 38

   Mercy Show-er 43

   Summary... 45

SECTION 2	51
Ascension Gifts & the Universal Body of Christ	51
Summary	64
SECTION 3	65
Appointments in the Local Body	65
What Was Appointed?	67
Why Were These Appointments Given?	68
Summary	83
SECTION 4	85
Apostles	85
Types of Apostles	90
Four Aspects of Apostolic Authority	103
Ministering Out of the Office	107
Apostolic Functions	110
Apostolic Manifestations	119
Other Earmarks of the Apostle	122
Prophets	126
The Prophetic Office & the Prophetic Appointment	126

Prophetic Manifestations 137

Evangelists 142

Philip the Evangelist 142

Paul & Barnabas Evangelizing 146

Timothy and the Work of an Evangelist 150

Evangelistic Manifestations 151

Teaching Pastors 156

An Overview 156

Teaching Pastor Manifestations 166

Comparing the Gifts 169

SECTION 5 171

Church Government 171

An Overview 171

Spiritual Territories 187

Elders 189

An Overview 189

Bishops/Overseers 196

Deacons 204

What are YOU called to do?.. 209

Works Cited.. 212

Acknowledgment

Few people modeled the life and role of an apostle like Rev. David Finley. Now retired, he labored over 30 years with the International Church of the Foursquare Gospel as a church rebuilder and planter. With his wife Barbara, they raised four sons who are all faithful to the venue God has placed them in. Serving with Dave was an honor. He was not into titles, but into faithful service. That is something we all need to model. Thank you, Dave.

II

Preface

Early in the history of the church, the strength and power of the apostolic office were wrested away from the church and replaced with a model that is the predominant model today - that of "pastor-centric" churches and ministries. The Spirit of the Lord has, in the last few years, been bringing about a correction to that flawed system of government—one which was never ordained by the Lord but nonetheless has been in operation for millennia.

You may question the necessity of discussing it since, as the old saying goes, "If it ain't broke, don't fix it!" But I propose to you that it is broken, and has been for so long that we've grown accustomed to it. We've accepted it with all its shortcomings and limitations when we did not have to. We have a guidebook to show us the pattern, but we have ignored it. This book will no doubt ruffle some feathers and perhaps anger you so much that you will put the book down and dismiss me as a kook, but I challenge you to read all the way through this book from the beginning to the end before making your determination. Do not read a little portion of this book and decide you know the whole story. For those of you who are pastors, it would be like one of your parishioners listening to only ten minutes of your sermon and deciding he knew all you were trying to convey. I hope I do make you mad enough to begin making the necessary changes so the church can return to its right footing. We are centuries behind where we should be, so change must begin now! It is not too late.

Author and Pastor Jim Wies made the following point in his book, *His Glorious House*:

> *It is my belief that as we see the culmination of the ages and the glorious Church emerging, it will be a Church that has all of its "body parts" functioning, including the "five-fold" leadership "vital organs." And as such, it will move in apostolic power and structure, prophetic clarity, evangelistic fervor, pastoral care, and nurture, and be fed on insight and understanding from the teaching ministries in the Church. But it will only become that, as it stays in right relationship to the Head of the Body, which is Christ Jesus. And when we see JESUS fully manifested in His Body, we will then see the mystery of God's*

> *destiny for humanity realized, and a people made ready to transition into the age to come. (Wies, 78)*[1]

His points are valid. I have a 4-cylinder Honda Accord. If I were trying to go somewhere with only three of the four cylinders firing, I would be neither be efficient, nor effective. The church has functioned similarly. Why is it that of the Ascension Gifts (Ephesians 4:11), the one that is discussed the least in the entire New Testament—the pastor—is the one we have elevated the most in our current church structures. On the other hand, the Ascension Gift most dominant in the New Testament the apostolic has been the least recognized and honored in our current church structure. Only in the last few years has that begun to change. May this book bring clarity and be a catalyst for a course correction in the body of Christ.

---

[1] Wies, *His Glorious House*, 78.

Introduction
A Fresh Look at 1 Corinthians 12

When I was a small child, I always enjoyed stories of hidden treasure. One of the earliest books I recall was "The Treasure of Doughnut Island," a little hardback book with a brown cover. It was my first multi-chapter book, and it was about finding treasure on this little doughnut-shaped island. Of course, like most young boys I also enjoyed pirate stories and their tales of adventure on the high seas. Even now, I enjoy a good movie about treasure hunting, so it should serve as no surprise that one-day several years ago while studying this passage of scripture, the Holy Spirit had me take note of a few things and proceed on a treasure hunt with Him.

Gifted with an ability to look at a passage of Scripture and break the passage down into the various components of the Scripture; it was in this way that the Holy Spirit began to show me some things. As with any revelation, you must be willing to allow the Holy Spirit to "stretch" you a bit because rarely does revelation fit into our tidy little molds. Revelation always brings revolution! Never should we seek revelation for its own sake, nor should we seek revelation that supersedes the Word of God. The Holy Spirit, however, may very well show us things that are beyond our comfort zone. We must be willing to set aside our preconceptions to embrace the things Holy Spirit is showing us. It is in this way that Holy Spirit began to teach me that day.

As I read 1 Corinthians 12, he began to point out to me the unique things Paul was writing about. I will be quoting primarily from the New King James Version. Remember where you find words in *italics* those were usually words the translators added in an attempt to clarify the passage. Sometimes it worked, but often it did not. Also, I have used James Strong's Expanded Exhaustive Concordance of the Bible for the definition of man words. When that occurs, these instances will be referenced in the footnotes. Here is that passage (beginning in verse 1) with my clarifications included in brackets [ ].

> [1]Now concerning spiritual *gifts*, brethren, I do not want you to be ignorant.
>
> Now concerning spiritual matters, My brothers, I would have you not to be clueless.

²Ye know that ye were Gentiles, carried away unto these dumb idols, even as ye were led.

²You know that you were pagans, following mute idols however they wished to lead you.

³Therefore I make known to you that no one speaking by the Spirit of God calls Jesus accursed, and no one can say that Jesus is Lord except by the Holy Spirit.

Here is where Holy Spirit had me slow down. He said to notice WHO was doing WHAT.

⁴Now there are diversities [*diairesis*²] of gifts [*charisma*³], but the same **Spirit**.

⁵And there are differences [*diairesis*] of ministries [*diakonea*⁴], but the same **Lord**.

---

² Strong, G1243. *diairesis* – varieties, distinctions.

³ Strong, G5483. *charisma* - a (divine) *gratuity*, a (spiritual) *endowment*, that is, or a miraculous *faculty:* - gift.

⁴ Strong, G1249. *diakonea - attendance* (as a servant); *aid*, (official) *service* (especially of the Christian teacher, or technically of the *diaconate*): minister (-ing, -tration, -try), office, relief, service (-ing).

> ⁶And there are diversities [*diairesis*] of activities [*energema*⁵], but it is the same **God** who works all in all.

I noticed that all three members of the Godhead were involved in these various distributions. No one had ever pointed that out to me before. He indicated to me that the giver and the "gift" were clues to what they were about. As I meditated on these thoughts, Holy Spirit asked me, "Where else do you find lists in the New Testament?" I immediately recalled Ephesians 4 where the Ascension Gifts are mentioned, and then I recalled Romans 12 where Paul had a listing of seven different things. I would not have to look very far to see the next list. No, it was not in the next few verses, but it was at the end of the same chapter I was studying. Let us continue with chapter 12.

> ⁷But the manifestation [*phanerosis*⁶] of the Spirit is given to each one for the profit *of all*.

He pointed out that the next list was not comprised of the "gifts of the Spirit" referred to in verse 4, but was different. These

---

⁵ Strong, G1754. *energema* - an *effect:* - operation, working.

⁶ Strong, G5319. *phanerosis* - *exhibition,* an *expression,* a *bestowment:* - manifestation.

nine things Paul discussed starting in verse 8 were "gifts" (the Greek word "*didomai*"), but not "gifts" (*charisma*) as mentioned in verse 4. Paul then begins the list of these nine manifestations of the Holy Spirit. (We'll deal with each of them more thoroughly later).

> ⁸For to one is given [*didomai*[7]] through the Spirit the word of wisdom; to another the word of knowledge through the same Spirit; ⁹to another faith by the same Spirit; to another gifts [*charismas*] of healings by the same Spirit; ¹⁰to another the working of miracles; to another prophecy; to another discerning of spirits; to another *different* kinds of tongues; to another the interpretation of tongues: ¹¹but one and the same Spirit works all these things, distributing individually to each one as He wills.

We need to notice **who** is giving **what**, to **whom** it is given, *and* the context in which it is given. Paul notes:

- Diversities of **gifts** (*charisma*) but the same **Spirit** (Holy Spirit)
- Diversities of **ministries** (*diakonos*), but the same **Lord** (Jesus)

---

[7] Strong, G1325. *didomai* - to give, bestow, bring forth, grant.

- Diversities of **activities** (*energema*), but the same **God**

In each of these three segments a part of the Godhead is giving something:

- Holy Spirit is giving *charismas* (graces) – these are not the same as the manifestations listed in 1 Corinthians 12:8-10
- Jesus is giving services/ministries (hence the term "ministry gifts")
- God is giving operations, workings or placements.

Where in the New Testament do we find the different parts of the Godhead giving things?

Jesus in Ephesians 4

Holy Spirit in Romans 12

God the Father in 1 Corinthians 12:29-31

An Overview

Here is a brief overview of where we will be going and what we will be discovering in this book:

1 Corinthians 12 is talking about the "manifestations" of the Spirit, but the real "gifts" of the Spirit are in Romans 12. These are the distinctions in personality and motivation given by the Holy Spirit to the individual believer. They are not given to the body of Christ as a whole – just to each individual.

Jesus, in Ephesians 4, is distributing differing graces to the body of Christ (universal); the ascension gifts of apostle, prophet, evangelist, pastor, and teacher.

God the Father, in 1 Corinthians 12:28-31, is placing within the local church (ecclesia) ministries to the local assembly to enable them to function.

Distribution	**Recipient**	**Giver**	**Scripture**
Gifts (charisma)	Individual Believer	Holy Spirit	Romans 12
Ministries	The body of Christ Universal	Jesus Christ	Ephesians 4
Appointments	Local Body of Christ	God the Father	1 Corinthians 12

In understanding these three differentiations, we must understand the context of the gift and the recipient. The local church has need of certain operations, the individual believer has need of certain things in his or her life, and the body of Christ at large have need of specific ministries. Understanding the scope of the ministry gifts or the operations will help us understand better how the Godhead intended them to function in the earth.

Some have viewed the listing in 1 Corinthians 12 as overlapping of Ephesians 4. However, I believe a study of the context will validate that it is, in fact, different. That is not to say that those called to one or more of the Ascension Gifts of Ephesians 4 are not also locally placed in accordance with 1 Corinthians 12. It is likely that we have both an overlap and at the same time a distinction between the two.

Contemporary Examples

At the risk of seeming to use my experience to validate scripture instead of the other way around, let me just mention a few modern day examples of men and women that might help explain this better.

Reinhard Bonnke

Many are familiar with Evangelist Reinhard Bonnke who holds mass crusades throughout Africa and India (now in America). His anointing is a continental anointing in that he has exercised a degree of spiritual authority throughout the continent of Africa. His ministry builds the local churches by providing an influx of new believers through the crusades he conducts (some with more than one million in attendance). Evangelist Bonnke, however, does not function in a local church. That is not to say that he does not support or attend a local church, but the focus of his ministry is outside the four walls of the local church. His ministry is to a larger segment of the population than is typical of the local church. Now, his associate Daniel Kolenda is continuing the ministry's focus on Africa while Evangelist Bonnke focuses on America.

Kenneth Copeland

A recognized prophet for approximately fifty years, Kenneth Copeland, with his wife Gloria, has served the body of Christ at large through his worldwide ministry. Although a local church is based on the grounds of their ministry headquarters in central Texas, their ministry is not limited to the local body at Eagle

Mountain International Church (EMIC). Their scope of ministry is much broader. He is not the pastor of the church at Eagle Mountain. Those duties fall to his son-in-law, George Pearson. Although that is the Copeland's home church, their ministry extends *from* Eagle Mountain International Church, not merely *to* Eagle Mountain International Church.

Lester Sumrall

The late Lester Sumrall, who functioned as an apostle (although he disdained titles) throughout the earth, carried an international authority that few men in modern times have carried. His international ministry impacted millions of people throughout the globe. Although Dr. Sumrall pastored a local body at South Bend, Indiana, his ministry extended far beyond the walls of that local church. That local body was merely part of his ministry base of operations. Because of his appointment as the founding pastor of the local church in South Bend, Dr. Sumrall was, according to 1 Corinthians 12:28, the local apostle of that house as well as an apostle internationally. He was responsible for churches being established throughout the earth in some form or fashion.

Derek Prince

The late Derek Prince functioned as a teacher to the body of Christ. God used his intellect coupled with his sensitivity to Holy Spirit to bring much understanding to the body of Christ. Although he died several years ago, the ministry he established continues unabated around the globe as his seemingly timeless teachings help bring understanding to the body of Christ around the globe.

Analyzing the Passage

In this book, we are going to look at:

- The Giver – Who gave it?
- The Gift – What was given?
- The Giftee (Recipient) – Whom was it given to?
- The Scope – Who is impacted by the gift?
- The Purpose – Why is it given?

…differences of ministries, but the same Lord

- Giver – Jesus
- Gift – Apostles, prophets, evangelists, pastors, teachers
- Giftee – select individuals

- Scope – The Universal body of Christ
- Purpose – Equip the saints for the work of the ministry

…diversities of activities, but the same God

- Giver – God
- Gift –Apostles, prophets, teachers, workers of miracles, gifts of healings, helps, governments, tongues, interpretation of tongues
- Giftee – select individuals in the body
- Scope – The Local Church
- Purpose – To enable the local church to function properly

Corresponding Grace

Whether your assignment is local, regional, national, or international, God gives corresponding grace. Kenneth Copeland will tell you he is not graced to pastor a body of believers. Yet his son-in-law is. We have to recognize the scope of our ministry and function within it. Many who have been called pastor have a much broader scope of ministry ahead of them, but because they have not embraced the apostolic paradigm of ministry or do not understand it, they have yet to step into that scope of ministry and the power behind it.

Several years ago a friend founded a local church. Because he had been raised in a traditional Pentecostal church setting, the term "pastor" was all he knew. He was almost completely unaware of the apostolic paradigm. However, God took him on an educational journey, and within a couple of years, he came to a new understanding of his appointment in that local body as the local apostle, not the "pastor" in the sense he had been taught. Once he embraced this new perception, his ministry went to the next level. This man now is in the processing of establishing a new work in a nearby city and has his sights set on establishing yet another work once the second one is stabilized. Functioning in an apostolic overseer role, this man is growing into a broader apostolic role than he ever envisioned. The first work he established has been turned over to his son to take care of while he and his team move to the second work. This man is actually stepping from the local apostolic role into a regional role, and it is exciting to see. He is experiencing an overlapping of the Ascension Gifts with the Local Appointments of 1 Corinthians 12.

In America, the church is based on a pastor-centric paradigm. However, I have a question to pose to those reading this: "Where can you find a pastor-centric church in the New Testament?" Secondly, "Whom can you name that was actually called as a 'pastor' in the New Testament?"

I am sure I just blew some of you out of the water with those two questions!

Now, before you close this book and dismiss it, consider for a moment: Who in the New Testament was referred to as Pastor? Whom can you say was identified as a pastor in the entire New Testament?

We in America, have made this model into such a proverbial sacred cow, it has been hard for us to consider any other option. We have based our church model on the typology of 'the sheep and shepherd' and not necessarily on the model of the New Testament.

Historically, in America, the black church has had a much better understanding of the apostolic-centered local church and has been much quicker to embrace an apostolic paradigm. They, as a group, embraced the terms "apostle" and "prophet" much sooner than the typical Anglo church in America. In fact, the Church of God in Christ, the nation's largest Pentecostal denomination, lists Dr. Charles E. Blake as their Presiding Bishop and Chief Apostle on their website (www.cogic.org).[8]

As you continue to read, I will demonstrate from scripture what I am talking about. I will also help answer the questions I posed a few moments ago. By the way, only one person in the entire New Testament can be verified as having been called as a "pastor." Can you figure out who that person is?

---

[8] "The Presiding Bishop."

SECTION 1

Motivational Gifts & The Individual Believer

Romans 12:6-8 is where we will find what the Holy Spirit was distributing in 1 Corinthians 12. The context of this passage shows us that these distributions were to the **individual members** of the body of Christ – not to the local or universal body of Christ.

Let us look at the following passages:

> ³ For I say, through the grace [*charis*[9]] given [*didomai*] to me, to everyone, who is among you, not to think of himself more highly than he ought to think but to think soberly, as God has dealt with each one a measure of faith. Romans 12:3

---

[9] Strong, G5483. *charisma* - a (divine) *gratuity,* a (spiritual) *endowment,* that is, or a miraculous *faculty:* - gift.

Paul is instructing the believers to understand that they are not to be high-minded. Everyone is different for a reason. Notice the words in brackets. You'll see these again in Ephesians 4.

> ⁴For as we have many members in one body, but all the members do not have the same function.

In this analogy, Paul is describing how our human bodies have all kinds of parts, and each part has a particular function. The big toe cannot do what the knee can do, and the knee certainly cannot do for the body what an ear can do.

> ⁵so we, *being* many, are one body in Christ, and individually members of one another.

Paul goes on to describe that in the same way, each believer makes up a part of the body of Christ and that each part of the body is merely that—part of a greater whole. In 1 Corinthians 12, you'll find Paul using a similar analogy which we will look at a little later.

Several years ago Dr. Marilyn Hickey wrote a book on "Motivational Gifts" or "Foundational Gifts" about this passage of Scripture. It has been revised and is now entitled "Know Your Ministry: Spiritual Gifts for Every Believer" and the current edition was co-written by her daughter Sarah Bowling. (Fortune)

(Hickey)" expound even further on these "motivational" gifts. Marilyn Hickey describes what she means by "motivational":

> *because they correspond to people's underlying inclinations and preferences, as well as to their special abilities, for serving the body of Christ and others.*[10]

What motivates you? What makes you "tick?" Some of us are extroverts, while others are introverts. Characteristics such as these can be seen in the following passage as Paul wrote:

> [6]Having then gifts differing according to the grace that is given to us, *let us use them:*[11]

Each of us has gifts [*charismas*] that differ according to the grace [*charis*] given to us. Each part has a defining grace to it. Each individual has a particular grace upon them. Each of us brings something different, but vital, to the table. Although the last portion of that verse says, *"let us use them,"* this attempt to clarify the verse by the translators may not have done so. These graces are not "things;"instead, they make us who we are. They are part of our makeup, and they bring an incredible diversity to

---

[10] Hickey, Marilyn. Know Your Ministry (Kindle Locations 63-64). Whitaker House. Kindle Edition.

[11] I Corinthians 12:6 (emphasis original)

the body of Christ that is needed. It is indeed understandable that we do not want everyone else to be just like us. We appreciate the uniqueness and benefit from it. On the next page, we will begin to look at these motivational giftings.

Prophetic Perceiver

Paul then begins to define the different graces. Remember in 1 Corinthians 12:4 "diversities of gifts [*charisma*], but the same Spirit...." Here in Romans 12, he begins to list the various *charismas*. The first of these is prophecy, or, as the Fortunes describe in their book, "perceivers."

> Prophetic Perceiver - Insight into Body of Christ, sees both good and evil. Typically sees only black and white – no grey.

> [6]...if prophecy, *let us prophesy* in proportion to our faith.

This verse would better read:

> "...if prophetic, perception, in proportion to our faith."

Have you ever noticed people who were rather prophetic in nature and often everything to them was black or white, with no room for gray? These are prophetic people, but that does not mean they are prophets. Let me make that distinction. Paul in Romans 12 is not referring to offices in which we operate, but graces, or giftings that define our personality.

We often lump all the uses of prophecy into one pile and do a disservice to the motivation, gift, office, and ministry of the prophet by the lack of distinction. Notice that though the phrase "*let us prophecy*" is in italics, it does not clarify the passage and ay even muddy it. In that passage we are *not* instructed to prophesy; rather the one with this motivational leaning is to live prophetically out of the grace to do so. The Fortunes say it this way:

> ***Perceiver****, one who clearly perceives the will of God. We have purposely chosen this word rather than the word "prophet" to avoid confusion since the same root word is also used in the two other categories of gifts*[12].

Remember, Romans 12:3 tells us that each man has been given a "measure of faith" and the lifestyle of prophetic perception operates on faith—faith that should be continuously growing in one's life. Realize too, that in this passage he is not referring to what we often call the "gift of prophecy." (We will discuss this a little later.) With maturity often comes fine-tuning of one's giftings/strengths/abilities along with confidence in using/operating in them. It is the same with this prophetic

---

[12] Fortune, Katie (1987-10-01). Discover Your God Given Gifts (Kindle Locations 335-336). Chosen. Kindle Edition.

perception. Therefore, Paul's instruction that "If [you are a prophetic perceiver] operate on the level of your faith to do so!"

Common Characteristics of Prophetic Perceivers (should be developed):

- Express messages verbally
- Discerns motives of people - they are very insightful
- Identifies evil
- Experiences brokenness (often in intercession)
- Uses scripture validation
- Wants outward evidence
- Frank in speaking
- Concern for the program of God
- Wants people to point out their "blind spots."

Common Misunderstandings (Things to eliminate):

- Their frankness can be viewed as harshness
- Usually more interested in groups than individuals
- They often love gimmicks
- Their focus on right and wrong can be seen as intolerance
- They often emphasize public appearance (find it hard to have close friends)
- Sees black and white only! Rarely sees gray

Examples of Prophetic Perceivers:

- John the Baptist
- Noah
- Jonah
- Ezekiel
- John Bevere
- Franklin Graham

Marilyn Hickey points out: "People with the prophecy motivation see things in black and white.[13] People with the prophecy motivation are frank and direct. They are not afraid to point out weaknesses, and they are very eager to have their own weaknesses exposed, as well, so they can grow and mature[14]. Having this motivation does not, however, make one a prophet. Although that may be the case, it is not necessarily so. They are simply prophetically inclined. As a matter of fact, they may not exercise any of the prophetic manifestations of 1 Corinthians 12:8-10, but simply be very perceptive. Often these individuals

---

[13] Hickey, Marilyn (2012-06-25). Know Your Ministry (Kindle Location 165). Whitaker House. Kindle Edition.

[14] Hickey, Marilyn (2012-06-25). Know Your Ministry (Kindle Locations 167-168). Whitaker House. Kindle Edition.

are very focused on holiness and right living. They have little toleration for sin in their own lives or in the lives of others. Unless they temper their lack of tolerance with grace, they can be very destructive and bring harm to individuals and the body of Christ. They need to understand that not everyone is like them, nor is everyone supposed to be. We need the variety to help balance our own temperaments.

Server

Paul continues in verse 7:

> [7]...or ministry, let us use it in our ministering (serving).

Have you known people who always found themselves wanting to serve others? Perhaps it is a lady at church who always is helping out by doing the little things that are necessary. Perhaps it is the person who always makes sure the guests are taken care of. These people are natural servers. They gain great joy from serving others, and for them, it is rarely a burden.

> **Server** - Meets practical needs of the Church. Lives to serve. The last one to leave, always trying to clean up the kitchen.

In verse 7, Paul defines "ministry" [*diakonia*] (or serving) as the second in his listing of motivations. The Greek *diakonia*[15] is the word from which we also get the phrase "deacon." Yet, Paul

---

[15] Strong. G1249. *diakonea* - *attendance* (as a servant); *aid*, (official) *service* (especially of the Christian teacher, or technically of the *diaconate*): minister (-ing, -tration, -try), office, relief, service (-ing)

in this context is not referring to jobs in the church or the body of Christ at large. Some people are just naturally servant-hearted. You often see them at the end of a meeting straightening the chairs, or cleaning the restrooms or washing the dishes. This servanthood just flows out of them. You do not have to ask them to serve; you will more likely have to ask them not to—they may need to sit down and rest and let someone else step up to the plate. These individuals will often never say "no" to a request to help out. Leaders in the body need to remain watchful that these individuals do not burn themselves out while doing good. They are the "Martha's" in the room. They are often focused on the practical needs of a church whereas the prophetically inclined have their heart on the spiritual issues in the body. These practical individuals are often the glue that keeps local churches functioning—they keep the restrooms clean, the auditorium tidy and the floors swept or vacuumed. The prophetic people, on the other hand, are likely to not even see many of those things and will gladly let these servant-minded persons do the "non-spiritual" things.

Characteristics of Servers (should be developed):

- Knows their likes and dislikes
- Detects practical needs
- Meets needs quickly

- Has physical stamina
- Willing to use personal funds
- Needs sincere appreciation
- Wants to see a job done, does extra work if necessary
- Involved in a lot of activities because they cannot say no
- Likes short-range goals are often not organizers

Misunderstandings (Things to eliminate):

- May appear to be pushy
- Avoids red tape—will do it themselves
- Upset with others when they do not have the same motive
- Difficult to accept service from others
- Easily hurt if appreciation is not forthcoming
- The desire to help others can interfere with God's dealing with people
- Gets sidetracked with others' needs and may miss God
- Meeting practical needs is not spiritual, may miss spiritual needs

Examples of Servers:

- Martha
- Ruth
- Mary Magdalene

Teacher

Then, Paul instructs teachers to teach within the grace given.

...[7] he who teaches, in teaching.

These individuals naturally want to learn and help others learn and are very concerned with truth. Is what they hear accurate? Is it in context? Is it the truth? Teachers want things done right! They hate to see scriptures taken out of context and misused. They also want others to value what they teach as much as they do which, of course, is neither possible nor realistic. They find themselves having trouble dealing with exhorters who are likely to pull a scripture out of its context to make a point. We should all be truth-seekers, but teachers are likely to be more concerned with it than others. Individuals with this motivation are likely to find themselves in teaching settings because it so naturally flows from them and they love it so much.

> Teacher - Desires to get people into the Word, to clarify the truth of the Word. Does not tolerate the misuse of scripture well.

A friend of one of my daughters was helping some of her classmates study for final exams. It took no time at all for her to have everyone at the table prepared and listening to her drill the information into them and then help them grasp the concepts. This young lady intends to become a teacher.

Characteristics of Teachers (should be developed):

- Has a natural ability to teach
- Loves to study the Word of God
- Tests the knowledge of those who teach them
- Loves to do research
- Validates new information
- Teaches in a systematic manner
- Takes scriptural illustrations over personal illustrations
- Wants you to "prove it" if you say it

Misunderstandings (Things to eliminate):

- Emphasis on scriptural interpretation may eliminate practical application
- Research may seem to be dependent on study books
- Use of knowledge in testing people may seem to be pride
- Details of research may be unnecessary when teaching
- Often lack warmth

Examples of Teachers:

- Paul

- Derek Prince
- Marilyn Hickey
- Beth Moore

Up to this point, some would say Paul was talking about the Ascension Gifts because he talked about prophecy, and teaching, two items listed in Ephesians 4. However, it is at this point that Paul expands the list, so to speak. He instructs exhorters to exhort, givers, to give with simplicity (not making a big show of it), and those who rule to do so with diligence, and those that show mercy, he instructs to do it with cheerfulness.

Exhorter

⁸Or he that exhorts, on exhortation.

These are the coaches among us—those who can motivate us to press onward and upward. They are likely to be naturally "charismatic" individuals who, when they come into the room, everyone knows it. When speaking publicly, they may pull a verse of scripture out of its context to apply it to the issue at hand. This, of course, grates on the teacher-motivated people in the room, but it never seems to bother the exhorter. They see it as their mission in life to help people go forward. They often seem to be the natural-born leaders among us. They often are great preachers and can draw large crowds, but they can have a tendency to ignore personal holiness (which the prophetic individuals would want to address). They tend to see the big picture, rather than the details that make up that picture, and they will sacrifice accuracy when applying the Word of God to make their point. Yet we need them in the body of Christ.

They will motivate people to rally behind a cause, but, when done with one cause, they quickly move on to the next project.

> **Exhorter** - Stimulates spiritual growth, loves to counsel people. Is willing to take the Word out of context to make a point. This person is an encourager.

It is hard for them to maintain a long-term focus on any given project. They must surround themselves with those who are administrative to see tasks accomplished—especially those tasks which require a long-term commitment. If a building project is involved, they will often tire of it long before it is completed.

They are able to rally the troops often. However, these types of people may drive the teaching or the prophetically-inclined crazy because exhorters are naturally encouragers. Virtually everyone likes encouragers, while teachers and prophetic people can often be a little harder to get to know.

Characteristics of Exhorters (should be developed):

- Desires to see steps of action
- Wants practical application, not turned on to informational things
- Likes to teach on tribulation - always wants a spiritual lesson
- Likes individual acceptance
- Teaches human experience and relates it to the person
- Enjoys seeing people take steps of action
- Grieved with teaching that is not practical
- Delights in conferences and counseling
- Likes to be with people
- Is a good at coaching

Misunderstandings (Things to eliminate):
- Emphasis on steps of action may seem to over-simplify the problem
- Desires to win non-Christians by example
- Use of scripture for the practical application may take it out of context
- Abandons large projects before their completion

Examples of Exhorters:
- Peter
- Barnabas

Giver

...he that gives let him do it with simplicity (generosity).

Thank God for the givers! They often make a huge difference in the financial support of ministries in churches. They find great joy in utilizing their resources for the purposes of the Kingdom of God. While others may tend toward being miserly, these individuals thrive. When the instruction is given to give with "simplicity" or "generosity," (some translations say "liberality") the implication is two-fold; give simply and generously without strings attached, and without withholding unnecessarily. Often they are very entrepreneurial and have the ability to make money fairly easily in comparison to other people.

> Giver - Loves to give and see others give.

In one case I know of, a gentleman feels he is called to underwrite the expenses of the ministries his church is involved in. Since accepting this "calling," he has written 6-figure checks on multiple occasions and has made a huge impact on this church's ability to accomplish its goals and directives.

Characteristics (should be developed)

- Has the ability to make money—very entrepreneurial
- Desires to give to ministries

- Likes to motivate others to give
- Wants to meet needs others may have overlooked
- Enjoys meeting needs without pressure
- Experiences joy when his gift is an answer to prayer
- Depends on the Lord as his source
- Concerned that gift be of high quality
- Desires to feel a part of the ministries he gives to

Misunderstandings (Things to eliminate)

- The need to deal with large sums of money may seem carnal
- Sometimes desires to control the work - do not put strings on gift
- Their attempt to motivate others to give could appear stingy

Examples of Givers

- Abraham
- David Hodgson
- Robert Benedict

Paul spoke of giving with simplicity because an area of concern with givers is they sometimes want to dictate the management of the church and/or its financial affairs when they are *not* anointed for that arena, nor is it necessarily their responsibility. As they give, they must always give as unto the Lord and not unto men. They gain joy from giving and may even need to be restrained from giving at times. Typically, these kinds of people are not controlled by things, and they tend to prefer simplicity.

Ruler/Leader

Paul continues in the administrative arena of life in verse 8:

> ⁸...he that rules, with diligence; he that shows mercy, with cheerfulness.

You, no doubt, know people that are natural born leaders. Some say that everyone is a leader. However, neither scripture nor practice supports this view. No doubt, certain qualities of leadership can be developed and refined, but just watch any group of small children playing, and it won't take but a few moments to see a leader rise to the top. The other types of people all need leaders to help direct their efforts, which is why it is so important that each of us functions in our place of responsibility.

> Ruler - Sets goals and gets things done. Generally very fastidious. Attends to details. Doesn't care for spontaneity.

Marilyn Hickey & Sarah Bowling put it this way.

> *In Romans 12:8, the Greek verb for "to lead" is* proistemi. *This word means "to stand before, i.e. (in rank) to preside" or "to maintain, be over, the rule" (Strong, G4291). Rulers—who commonly function as*

> *organizers—stand in front because they have the ability to direct others. Through their God-given leadership ability, they facilitate tasks for the rest of the body of Christ. They know how to organize people and to help them develop to fulfill their purposes.*[16]

In a sense, they are similar to the teaching motivated person in that they like organization and are naturally good at it. Some of the other personality types need this strength in their lives, and it is often that an exhorter will have someone with administrative or organizational skills working by their side. For an exhorter, this can be especially helpful since they can often create chaos in their wake, being so focused on their exhorting.

In the Fortunes' book, they describe this type as:

> *Administrator, one who loves to organize, lead, or direct. Other words could be "facilitator" and "leader."*

In local churches and ministries, this ability is vital if that church or ministry wants to grow. Otherwise, the level of disorganization will determine the level of impact of the

---

[16] Hickey, Marilyn (2012-06-25). Know Your Ministry (Kindle Locations 716-719). Whitaker House. Kindle Edition.

organization. The principle of "faithful over much...ruler over much" comes into play here.

Another aspect of leadership is brought out in the instructions of Jethro (Moses father-in-law) to Moses concerning governing the children of Israel:

> [21] Moreover, you shall select from all the people able men, such as fear God, men of truth, hating covetousness; and place *such* over them *to be* rulers of thousands, rulers of hundreds, rulers of fifties, and rulers of tens. [22] And let them judge the people at all times. Then it will be *that* every great matter they shall bring to you, but every small matter they shall judge. So it will be easier for you, for they will bear *the burden* with you. Exodus 18:21-22

Within the leadership, gifting is the inherent ability of some to work with smaller groups, while others may be best suited for larger groups. Their gifting will make room for them[17].

We need those who can help us steward our resources and ministries. Nehemiah and Joseph are possibly the best examples of this kind of person; Nehemiah as he organized the rebuilding

---

[17] Proverbs 18:16

of the walls of Jerusalem and Joseph as he served as the prime minister of Egypt.

Characteristics of Leaders (should be developed):

- Ability to see the overall picture and make long-range goals
- Motivated to organize only what he is asked to do
- Desires to complete the task quickly and not put it off
- Aware of resources available before starting a job
- Has the ability to know who can do a job
- Assumes responsibility if no one else is around
- Endures reactions from others—even when they do not approve
- Loves to see a completed task
- Desires to move on to a new challenge

Misunderstandings (Things to eliminate):

- Ability to delegate may appear to be laziness
- Willingness to endure reactions from others may appear as callousness
- Has a tendency to neglect to tell others why he has set up the goal
- Views people as resources instead of seeing them as people

Examples of Leaders

- Moses
- Joseph
- Nehemiah

Mercy Show-er

Have you noticed that some people are just naturally compassionate? These people feel the pain of the hurting deeply and often find themselves in counseling situations or intercessory settings where they pray for or minister to those in need. Without these individuals, the body of Christ would in certain respects face difficulty in living out the love of God to the world.

> Mercy - Feeler of the Body, feels emotional needs. Basically the opposite of a perceiver. Is probably run by their heart, not their head. Can see the grey and does not see the black and white as easily.

Marilyn Hickey points out:

> *...those who have the foundational gift of mercy love people and are happy to show them compassion. It is not burdensome to them; rather, they desire to reach out to those who are afflicted, wounded, and in need*[18].

---

[18] Hickey, Marilyn (2012-06-25). Know Your Ministry (Kindle Locations 831-832). Whitaker House. Kindle Edition.

Quite often you will find the prophetic/perceiver type coupled with the mercy show-er/compassionate type. The challenge this type faces is softness toward sin. Often those in the pastoral ministry are this kind of person, and their challenge is being able to deal with tough situations within the church. They are simply not emotionally equipped for these scenarios. Many times you will see the tougher prophetic/ perceiver married to the softer compassionate/mercy show-er. This brings a needed balance to the marriage. In parenting, the prophetic person will tend to be harder in disciplinary matters, while the compassionate person may tend to be too soft in those areas.

Characteristics of Mercy Show-ers (should be developed):

- Exhibit great compassion
- Are willing to sacrifice resources to help someone
- Not geared toward confrontation
- Can easily find themselves in intercession
- Drawn naturally to the downcast and brokenhearted

Misunderstandings (Things to eliminate):

- Avoidance of firmness may appear as weakness
- Some believe they are led by emotions, not reason
- Attraction to those upset can be taken the wrong way (Should be men to men and women to women)

- Are usually bad time managers
- Willingness to serve leaves them unwilling to confront when necessary
- Find it hard to exhibit "tough love."
- Often taken advantage of.

Examples of Mercy Show-ers:

- Hosea
- John

Summary

Marilyn Hickey and Sarah Bowling give a good synopsis of this passage of scripture with very practical insights about each. I would recommend you purchase their book, *Know Your Ministry*[19].

Each of these seven types of people has a uniqueness that needs to be embraced by the others. Clearly, no one fits into only one of these types. Often, one of the seven will be predominant with secondary tendencies from one or more of the other areas. It is an interesting thing to note that often a prophetic person will marry a compassionate person, or an exhorter will marry a

---

[19] Marilyn Hickey & Sarah Bowling (2012), *Know Your Ministry* (ISBN: 978-1603745024) Whitaker House (2012).

teacher or some other mixture. The old adage, "opposites attract" is often quite true. Not only do they attract, but they also tend to bring balance to relationships and to people. Prophetic people need to understand that not everything on the planet is black or white and that a bit of gray actually does exist. The realization that I likely just upset a few ultra-prophetic people also proves my point. The ultra-prophetic among us need the tempering provided by the other types. In the same vein, the compassionate mercy show-er's need to understand that sin can continue unchecked forever if not dealt with at some point.

Although it would seem logical that prophetic people would also be prophets, the Godhead always has a way of mixing things up for us so that not everything is so predictable and "cut and dried." Prophetic people may be prophets, or they may be used prophetically, but it is not a guarantee, no more than a teacher being guaranteed that he or she would function in the office of the teacher.

Recognizing that God loves to interrupt our ways of thinking and mix things up a bit is helpful in working through the study of these things. Just when you think you've got it all figured out, God changes something or makes an exception of some sort. The following table[20] is taken from Don & Katie Fortune's book, "Discovering Your God-Given Gifts" and will help you see the bigger picture.

GIFT	DEFINITION	NEEDS MET	WHAT IT DOES
Perceiver	Declares the will of God	Spiritual	Keeps us centered on spiritual principles
Server	Renders practical service	Practical	Keeps the work of ministry moving
Teacher	Researches & teaches the Bible	Mental	Keeps us studying & learning
Exhorter	Encourages personal progress	Psychological	Keeps us applying spiritual truths
Giver	Shares material assistance	Material	Keeps specific needs provided for

---

[20] Fortune, Katie (1987-10-01). Discover Your God Given Gifts (Kindle Location 535). Chosen. Kindle Edition.

Administrator	Gives leadership & direction	Functional	Keeps us organized & increases our vision
Compassion Person or Mercy Show-er	Provides personal & emotional support	Emotional	Keeps us in correct attitudes & relationships

As we wrap up this segment, keep in mind the focus of these seven motivations or foundations as Marilyn Hickey also refers to them. They are what makes us "tick." We must learn to live out of who we are. These foundational gifts are what our entire life is built upon. We do what we do because we are who we are. With our uniqueness, we make up quite a menagerie of styles, preferences, and attitudes. It is a wonderful diversity through which the love of God can be demonstrated. As we value and celebrate our brothers and sisters, we will become richer and wiser.

	MOTIVATIONAL GIFTS
Giver	Holy Spirit
Gift	Motivations (perceiving, serving, teaching, exhorting, giving, leading, mercy-showing)
Giftee	Individual members of the body of Christ
Scope	Individual Believers
Purpose	Help believers understand how they are made—personality understandings

SECTION 2

Ascension Gifts & the Universal Body of Christ

Paul, in 1 Corinthians 12:5, refers to "diversities of administrations, but the same Lord." Lord, in this context, is referring to Jesus Christ, who is referred to as Lord throughout the New Testament and particularly in the writings of Paul. As I continued in my "classroom" with Holy Spirit, I followed His instructions to look at the "lists" mentioned in the New Testament. That instruction took me to Ephesians 4:11. To look at only that verse is to miss the context and the greater message so we will look at the larger context. I will quote the passage:

> ⁷But to each one of us grace was given according to the measure of Christ's gift. ⁸Therefore He says: "WHEN HE ASCENDED[21] ON HIGH, HE LED CAPTIVITY

---

[21] Where the term "Ascension Gifts" comes from.

CAPTIVE, AND GAVE GIFTS (*doma*[22]) TO MEN." ⁹(Now this, "HE ASCENDED"—what does it mean but that He also first descended into the lower parts of the earth? ¹⁰He who descended is also the One who ascended far above all the heavens that He might fill all things.) ¹¹And He Himself gave some *to be* apostles, some prophets, some evangelists, and some pastors and teachers, ¹²for the equipping of the saints for the work of ministry, for the edifying of the body of Christ, ¹³till we all come to the unity of the faith and of the knowledge of the Son of God, to a perfect man, to the measure of the stature of the fullness of Christ. Ephesians 4:7-13

As we see from this passage, we have still another word in Greek that is translated as "gifts" (*doma*). Each word has a slightly different meaning, and this particular word is only used four (4) times in the New Testament:

In the first two, Jesus has been speaking of prayer and finished with these promises:

---

[22] Strong. G1390. *doma* - from the base of G1325; a *present:* - gift.

> If you then, being evil, know how to give good **gifts** to your children, how much more will your Father who is in heaven give good things to those who ask Him! Matthew 7:11

> If you then, being evil, know how to give good **gifts** to your children, how much more will *your* heavenly Father give the Holy Spirit to those who ask Him!" Luke 11:13

The next time we see it is in Ephesians 4:8 when Paul is actually quoting from Psalm 68:18 which says,

> You have ascended on high; You have led captivity captive; You have received **gifts**[23] among men, Even *from* the rebellious, That the LORD God might dwell *there*. Psalm 68:18

Here is Paul's version:

> Therefore He says: "When He ascended on high, He led captivity captive, and gave **gifts** to men. " Ephesians 4:8

---

[23] Strong. H4979. *mattanah* - a present; specifically (in a good sense) a sacrificial offering - gift.

And the final time we see the word "*doma*" used in the New Testament is in Philippians 4:17.

> Not that I seek the **gift**, but I seek the fruit that abounds to your account.

Verses 9 and 10 speak of Jesus' activities between his crucifixion and resurrection and are not pertinent to our discussion so we will move past them. In the next verse, Paul writes of Jesus:

> And He Himself gave some *to be* apostles, some prophets, some evangelists, and some pastors and teachers. Ephesians 4:11

This grouping is often referred to as the "five-fold" ministry, but the sentence structure in neither Greek nor Aramaic support this. The pastors and teachers are more of a co-joined thought than separated offices. For that reason, I choose to refer to them as the "Ascension Gifts." Often this listing gets combined with the listing given by God the Father in 1 Corinthians 12:28-29, but that would be an incorrect compilation because of the scope of each grouping. In Ephesians 4 the scope is the body of Christ universally, whereas in 1 Corinthians 12:28-29, the scope is the local *ecclesia* (body) of Christ - i.e., the local church.

One who is an Ascension Gift apostle has an entirely different scope of ministry than a local apostle (1 Corinthians 12). Their level of influence is different as is their geographical degree of influence. They generally deal with larger segments of the body of Christ (i.e., regional, territorial, states, nations, people groups). Peter and Paul would have fit into this category as they were the apostles to the Jews and Gentiles respectively on a global scale. The following chart may help sort this out in your mind:

Holy Spirit	**Jesus**	**God the Father**
Romans 12	Ephesians 4	I Corinthians 12
Motivational Gifts	Ascension Gifts	Appointments
Body of Christ- Individually	Body of Christ- Universally	Body of Christ- Locally
Prophetic/Perceiving	Apostles	Apostles
Serving	Prophets	Prophets
Teaching	Evangelists	Teachers
Exhorting	Pastor-teacher	Workers of Miracles
Giving		Gifts of Healings
Ruling/Organizing		Helps
Mercy Showing		Governments
		Different Kinds of Tongues
		Interpretation of Tongues

Although we see what appears to be an overlap with the apostles in two categories and the prophetic in three categories, such is not the case. Because of the scope of each gift, they impact us in different ways.

Let me revert to another point I wanted to make. In Ephesians 4:7 Paul makes this statement:

> ⁷But to each one of us grace was given according to the measure of Christ's gift.

Each of these gifts (the apostle, prophet, evangelist, and pastor-teacher) have unique graces they impart to the body of Christ *(I will deal with each of these offices in more detail a bit later.)* If a church only sees or experiences the pastor-teacher gift, they miss out on the seer aspect of the prophetic gift or the "setting in order" aspect of the apostolic gift. By missing out on these other graces, the church can experience a sort of imbalance which will lead to other problems eventually. The local body of Christ needs to be exposed to the apostolic office, prophetic office, the evangelist's office, and the teaching/pastoral ministries that are non-local (or at least non-local for them).

We also have no New Testament pattern for the pastor to be the senior leadership of a local body of believers as we, particularly in America, have come to experience. Our pastor-centric model has created its own brand/set of problems, and in over forty years of ministry, I have witnessed these shortcomings. I recall wondering years ago where we this model came from when I did not see it in the book of Acts or anywhere else in the New Testament. This will be discussed more a bit later.

Another challenge with the pastor-centric model is the typical motivational gift mix involved. The pastor-centric model is rich in a compassion-motivational mix with good pastors being good listeners, yet they are often weak with regard to dealing with sin in the church and confronting situations that need a strong hand. The apostolic office, on the other hand, typically offers a gift mix that is more willing to confront sin and make hard decisions Often they are the prophetic/perceiver type. In Acts 5 we have a very dramatic example of the apostolic office dealing with sin in the church when Peter confronts Ananias and Sapphira, and they immediately died for having lied to the Holy Spirit. Paul, in Galatians 5:9 and 1 Corinthians 5:6 declared:

A little leaven leavens the whole lump.

Peter understood that the toleration of sin in the church would result in its ultimate propagation in the church. Paul, in 1 Corinthians 5, we find forcefully addressing the situation of the man sleeping with his father's wife. He instructed the leaders of the church to turn the man over to Satan for the destruction of the flesh. This is the context in which Paul speaks of "a little leaven leavens the whole lump." The social fabric of the church could not endure the tolerance of such wickedness in its midst. Could it be that the contemporary church would have a much stronger voice in society if we had not so long tolerated sin in our own camps?

Let me give an illustration of a scenario I witnessed first-hand a few years ago:

> In a local church, we had just begun attending, a man in the church (one of the leaders) was found to have had multiple affairs with multiple married women in the church. He was also married during this time. When the adulterous situations came to light, the weakness of the pastor of the church came to light as well. He was a wonderfully compassionate teacher who was a great counselor, but this scenario required someone willing to confront the sin and cut it off—which he was unwilling to do. Instead, when the man was brought before the church, the pastor said, in essence, "We need to pray for _____. He is going through a hard time."

The sin was never addressed, the affected families were never given proper closure or counseling administered to them, and as a result, he was never brought to correction and so continued down the same path. Meanwhile, every one of the marriages that had been affected broke up, ending in divorce—the lives of the husbands, wives, and children shattered. By the way, most of these affairs occurred while the husbands were on deployment in the military.

This scenario should never have occurred—not merely the adultery, but the way it was handled. If the pastor was unable or unwilling to handle the situation effectively, then someone in authority over him should have been brought in to deal with it as forcefully as the situation warranted. Unfortunately, the "pastor" involved is no longer pastoring but was elected to the senior state leadership position in his denomination—an office requiring strong apostolic leadership. To my knowledge, he has not risen to the office, merely the position.

If you sense in my writing a bit of disdain for the improper handling of this situation by the pastor and the failure of both the church and the organization to deal effectively with it, you are correct. It should never have been allowed to occur. I do not like confrontation either, and if it is a situation larger than I feel competent to deal with, I will look to those in leadership above me for their assistance or intervention. Our pastor-centric model has failed us miserably in areas of church discipline. That must change!

Often the hierarchy of the denominations is based on a modified pastor-centric basis so the problem is merely exacerbated unless they elect individuals with a more apostolic mindset. As we continue through this book, we will cover some other aspects of the pastor-centric model vs. an apostolic paradigm. First, though, we need to delve into the first, in two of our lists, of the graces given to the church—that of the apostle.

We find in verses 12 and 13 of Ephesians 4 the reason for these Ascension Gifts:

> And he (Jesus) gave some apostles, and some prophets, and some evangelists, and pastors and teachers [12]for the equipping of the saints for the work of ministry, for the edifying of the body of Christ, [13]till

we all come to the unity of the faith and of the knowledge of the Son of God, to a perfect man, to the measure of the stature of the fullness of Christ. Ephesians 4:11-13

Jesus wants us to "grow up." He wants His body equipped to do the work of the ministry. One of the primary characteristics of the apostolic office is the equipping nature of it. They want to set forth both men and women into ministry. That is a large part of their ministry responsibility. We see from Paul's example how he equipped Timothy and Titus, who later became apostles in their own right and replicated Paul's ministry by equipping others. The pastoral office as we have come to know it seems to be less concerned with equipping and more with maintaining. This mindset plays into the reluctance of some pastors to have evangelists or prophets, in particular, come to minister at their church. They do not want any upheaval. They often only want to develop and maintain a stable environment with as little trouble as possible. They want to experience "smooth sailing" which is understandable in one respect, but unrealistic in another.

The writer of the following proverb tells us the price of oxen:

Where no oxen *are,* the trough *is* clean; but much increase *comes* by the strength of an ox. Proverbs 14:4

What he did not say is as important as what he did say in this particular verse. Essentially, if no work is being done and no oxen are in the stalls, the stalls will remain clean. However, if you have oxen, and they are working, they will dirty up the tidy stalls. Work produces messes. Growth produces messes. If you don't want messes, then do not do anything, but if you want to see progress, understand that messes will develop.

Dr. Scott Reece, Senior Leader at New Hope Church-MGT in Moline, Illinois, gave this perspective in a Facebook blog post:

> *There is a fresh wind blowing through the kingdom, giving birth and resurrection to the 5-fold ministry in the church. The 5-fold ministry is a governmental structure and function, and churches that do not understand and make room for it easily become "pastor-centric," thus tipping the governmental scales out of balance and reducing the kingdom effectiveness (and growth) of the church.*
>
> *It's a New Testament governmental system that has been so misaligned over the years (by the enemy), that it threatens most when in reality it's the key to what you've been longing for. In the days to come, God is raising up a new breed of Kingdom-minded leaders,*

who will help the church find an appropriate and genuine, Spirit-filled comprehension of this biblical blueprint of life, health, growth, blessing, and accountability.

This is a starting point and will help you:

> *Apostles - Govern*
> *Prophets - Guide*
> *Evangelists - Gather*
> *Pastors - Guard*
> *Teachers - Ground*[24]

Dr. Reece formerly served as the District Superintendent for the Southeast District of the Foursquare[25] church and during his tenure helped steer that movement toward a more apostolic paradigm.

Unfortunately, the conventional forms of church government do not encourage the level of innovation that is common to the apostolic office. The deacons, elders, or advisory boards commonly direct the operations of many churches with the pastor being the 'front man,' so to speak. More on the apostolic

---

[24] Facebook/Scott Reece. Posted 5/14/2016.
[25] The International Church of the Foursquare Gospel, Los Angeles, California.

will be covered in Section 4 while more about church government will be covered in Section 5.

Summary

ASCENSION GIFTS	
Giver	Jesus Christ
Gift	Apostles, Prophets, Evangelists, Teaching Pastors
Giftee	Select Individuals
Scope	The Universal Body of Christ
Purpose	Equip the saints for the work of the ministry

SECTION 3

Appointments in the Local Body

APPOINTMENTS IN THE LOCAL BODY	
Giver	God
Gift	Apostles, Prophets, Teachers, Workers of Miracles, Gifts of Healings, Helps, Governments, Tongues, Interpretation of Tongues
Giftee	Select Individuals in the body
Scope	The Local Body of Christ
Purpose	Equip the saints for the work of the ministry on a local level

1 Corinthians 12:28 is our next passage of scripture, and the one Holy Spirit took me to next in my treasure hunt. It is accompanied by a couple more verses which will be included here:

> ²⁷Now you are the body of Christ, and members individually. ²⁸And God has <u>appointed²⁶ these in the church</u>: first apostles, second prophets, third teachers, after that miracle, then gifts of healings, helps, administrations, varieties of tongues. ²⁹Are all apostles? *Are* all prophets? *Are* all teachers? *Are* all workers of miracles? ³⁰Do all have gifts of healings? Do all speak in tongues? Do all interpret? (emphasis mine) 1 Corinthians 12:27-30

The setting is the ecclesia (local church) where God is appointing men and women to function within that body of believers. The first three: apostles, prophets, and teachers are distinct from the Ascension Gifts of Ephesians 4. If you remember the verse earlier in the book, we were looking at the things the Holy Spirit gave (Romans 12), the Lord Jesus gave (Ephesians 4), and God the Father gave (1 Corinthians 12:28). With the context being the local body of Christ (the *ecclesia*) he is describing the appointments/offices that should be a part of a thriving body of believers.

The Aramaic English New Testament[27] translates it this way:

---

[26] Strong. G5087. *tithami* - to place; appoint, bow, commit, conceive, give ordain, purpose, put, set (forth).

[27] AENT - 1 Corinthians 12:28

For Elohim has **placed** in His assembly. (emphasis mine)

The Weymouth Translation puts it nicely:

And by God's appointment, there are in the Church—first Apostles, secondly Prophets, thirdly teachers. Then come miraculous powers, and then the ability to cure diseases or render loving service, or powers of organization, or varieties of the gift of 'tongues.' 1 Corinthians 12:28[28]

One picture of this is that God looked at a local fellowship and saw vacancies in the leadership structure of it. For these various vacancies, he appointed from *within* the body people to fill the different positions. If they were not available locally, then he would bring them in from another locale. In some cases, he would have them drawn to Jesus, discipled in the church, and raised up and placed in that position.

What Was Appointed?

First apostles – delegated authority

Second prophets – forth-teller, seer, foreteller

---

[28] 1912 Weymouth New Testament (Public Domain)

Third teachers – instructor in righteousness

Miracles – worker of miracles

Gifts of healings – ministers of healing

Helps – relief (from a word that means to support, participate, aid)

Administrations/governments – to steer, pilotage, directorship

Varieties of tongues – one who ministers in various languages

Interpretation of tongues – one who interprets the languages ministered

Why Were These Appointments Given?

These men and women are endowed for the purpose of ministering within their realm in the local church and for the evangelism of the church to the community and the establishment of the Kingdom of God in their particular domain.

When was the last time you saw these recognized as appointments to the local church?

Local Apostles

Paul starts with "first apostles." The language structure clearly indicates a sort of hierarchy. I have heard many leaders attempting to "apologize" for their apostleship. In their vain attempts to appear humble, they disgraced the office to which they were called. We do not see a pattern of Paul downplaying his role, nor do we ever see him apologizing for acting like an apostle. He was not braggadocios[29] about it; he simply knew who he was and walked in it. Ironically I have heard few if any ever apologizing for being a "pastor" although no New Testament pattern exists for the "office" they purport to hold. (More on that later.)

Local Apostles (the term I use for this appointment) are those leaders designated by God to serve the local body they are appointed to. In our culture, they may use the culturally correct term of pastor, but if they walk in the strength of the apostolic anointing, they will not be deemed a "pastor" for very long. The motivational mix may be along the lines of Ruler/Prophetic or Ruler/Teacher, though no hard and fast rules apply. God likes to mix things up for us and keep us in absolute dependence upon

---

[29] boastful - "braggadocious." *Collins English Dictionary - Complete & Unabridged 10th Edition*. HarperCollins Publishers. 02 May. 2016. <Dictionary.com http://www.dictionary.com/browse/braggadocious>.

him. More will be discussed concerning Local Apostles in Section 4, but let us continue with the appointments in the local body.

>...secondarily prophets. 1 Corinthians 12:28

Local Prophets

The second appointment Paul delineates is that of a Local Prophet. (I use the prefix "Local" to differentiate between the 1 Corinthians 12:28 "appointments" and the Ephesians 4 "ascension gifts"). This second position of the prophet in the local body is in keeping with the indication that the apostles and prophets were foundational offices[30]. Local churches need the foundation these two offices provide. Again these two offices are not known for their tolerance of "sin in the camp," but rather will hit it head on if necessary. The goal of dealing with any sin situation in a church is always restoration, but often it will involve "tough love." It will take the necessary steps to rid the body of the encroaching cancer of sin.

The prophet office will also help in securing the proper direction for the church. As "seers" into the purposes of God,

---

[30] Ephesians 2:20 having been built on the foundation of the apostles and prophets, Jesus Christ Himself being the chief corner*stone*.

they can ascertain what God is saying, but they lack the necessary authority to establish those purposes in the local body firmly. That authority rests with the apostolic leader–the senior leadership position in the church.

When the apostolic office was replaced by appointed "pastors" centuries ago around the time of Constantine, it was not merely a slight change to how "church was to be done;" rather, it was a paradigm shift. For whatever reason, the strength of the apostolic office was wrested away from the church and replaced by "pastors" to serve as "shepherds over the flock." The senior leadership was never supposed to be "shepherds of a flock," but more like an admiral over an aircraft carrier[31] where ministries are developed, trained and deployed; where the focus is on advancing the Kingdom and forcefully destroying the works of hell in the earth.

The apostolic model had been functioning very effectively in spite of a great deal of persecution since the establishment of the church by Jesus. Of particular note was their financial strength. As we see in the book of Acts, the believers contributed generously to the needs of the widows and orphans (two

---

[31] TheFreedomOutpost.net (Stephen Thompson) https://youtu.be/WeSr_F7b7D8

particular groups of people that, in Roman eyes, were "non-persons.") The church modeled a different approach to these outcasts of society to the point that Rome eventually changed how they viewed both the outcasts and the Christians. If you can imagine a movement that consisted of a strong leadership hierarchy which maintained great treasuries and effective distribution systems, and which was increasing exponentially in the earth. This got the attention of Constantine. Remember, these churches did not have property to maintain; rather the believers met "house to house" and in public spaces for their larger gatherings. Constantine was likely advised that "if you can gain control of the leadership of this movement, you will also gain control of their finances." In the process of gaining control, Christians were eventually forbidden to meet house to house but instead met in the approved venues (often pagan temples that had been converted to "churches"). These churches were led by those approved by Constantine or his supporters and so they "toed the company line" preaching what was approved and not making trouble for the Emperor or for themselves. Such was the eventual takeover of the church by the pastor-centric model that is still predominant today.

It was not long afterward that the Dark Ages ensued. Could we possibly find some degree of correlation? The expansive growth of the church in some ways slowed down, but in other ways, the "church" seemed to grow. Since Christianity was no longer outlawed, it became the fashionable thing to be considered a "Christian." Whether true conversions or politically expedient ones, we will not know anytime soon, but God was not undone by this series of developments regarding the church. He caused it to progress in other ways.

Local Teachers

Now back to our study in 1 Corinthians 12. Paul next declares:

> ...third teachers.

The importance of the teacher cannot be underestimated, and regarding the local body, this is likely where we would also find those who serve in the role that today we refer to as pastors. They provide feeding and nurturing of the body and focus on establishing the believers in truth. We see in Acts 13:1,

> Now <u>in the church that was at Antioch,</u> there were certain **prophets** and **teachers**: Barnabas, Simeon who was called Niger, Lucius of Cyrene, Manaen who had

been brought up with Herod, the tetrarch, and **Saul.** (emphasis mine)

In this passage, Saul (Paul) and Barnabas are listed among the prophets and teachers, and as we will see in the next few verses, they began the apostolic portion of their ministry:

> ²As they ministered to the Lord and fasted, the Holy Spirit said, "Now separate to Me Barnabas and Saul for the work to which I have called them." ³Then, having fasted and prayed, and laid hands on them, they sent *them* away. ⁴So, being sent out by the Holy Spirit, they went down to Seleucia, and from there they sailed to Cyprus. Acts 13:2-4

Saul (our Paul) began his apostolic ministry at this junction having served as a prophet and/or teacher. Often those in apostolic office have gone through the ranks, so to speak, in their journey of faith. It is evident that Paul functioned as a teacher on the local level (See Acts 13:2-4 above) along with a probable overlap with the Ascension Gift of Teacher since his teaching ministry was not restricted to one locale or region.

It would stand to reason that any of the Ascension Gifts ministries could function on an international level, as well as regional level and possibly other "levels" that have not been distinguished in this book. Also, it seems entirely probable that these Ascension Gift offices would not necessarily be restricted to functioning within the body of Christ, or in solely a ministry setting, but that they could also extend to the marketplace, where men and women serve as apostles and prophets, evangelists and pastor-teachers in that setting.

Miracles

Following the teacher, Paul describes "miracles" or "miracle workers" among the appointments in the local church. Rarely has this appointment been utilized in the local church to my knowledge. It, like the manifestation of working of miracles, is often treated like fine china that we only bring out on special occasions. We have not experienced the benefit of this appointment among us because we have not honored it. If churches were to do so, might their evangelistic thrust increase dramatically?

The fact that these were appointments within the local church does not restrict their operation outside of the local church. On the contrary, Jesus made clear what he wanted to do and how he wanted the Kingdom of Heaven to invade the earth when he gave these instructions to his disciples in Matthew:

> And when He had called His twelve disciples to *Him*, He gave them power *over* unclean spirits, to cast them out, and to heal all kinds of sickness and all kinds of disease. Matthew 10:1

Instead of tolerating infirmity and workers of darkness among us, we should cast them out and release the miraculous power of God in those situations. A few verses later he says,

> [7]And as you go, preach, saying, 'The kingdom of heaven is at hand.' [8]Heal the sick, cleanse the lepers, raise the dead, cast out demons. Freely you have received, freely give. Matthew 10:7-8

If the church was known for raising the dead instead of burying them, how do you think society would view the church? Instead of portraying Christians as bigoted, weak and ignorant, the world may be less tempted to degrade us.

Examples in Acts are:

- Stephen – Acts 6:8
- Philip – Acts 8:13
- Paul – Acts 19:11; Romans 15:19; 1 Corinthians 2:4
- Unknown others – Galatians 3:5

It is above and beyond the manifestation of the working of miracles (1 Corinthians 12:9). It is above and beyond the general authority to work miracles in Jesus' name.

Gifts of healings

These individuals are ministers of healings (supernaturally). I am not referring to doctors, nurses, or naturopaths. These gifts of healings are of a supernatural nature and supersede the normal processes of healing that we all can experience. It is an appointment in the local body to facilitate healing manifestations in that body. It is often above and beyond the typical manifestation of the gifts of healing (1 Corinthians 12:9), and it is above and beyond the command to lay hands on the sick or the general ministering of healing that any believer can do

Helps

Helps – relief (from a word that means to support, participate, aid). Those persons anointed and appointed to aid in the work of the local body. Romans 16:3-4 describe Priscilla and Aquila as Paul's "helpers in Christ Jesus." Romans 16:9 speaks of Urbane, his helper in Christ, and Stachys "my beloved." In 1 Corinthians 16:15-16 Paul writes:

> I urge you, brethren—you know the household of Stephanas, that it is the firstfruits of Achaia, and *that* they have devoted themselves to the ministry of the saints—that you also submit to such, and to everyone who works and labors with *us*.

Apparently, these individuals had Paul's respect and carried a degree of authority.

Dr. Buddy Bell has traveled extensively across the globe teaching on the "gift of helps." Unfortunately, some have taken his teachings and made the erroneous statements such as, "if you are not in the 'five-fold' [meaning Ephesians 4:11 giftings], then you are in the gift of helps." I hope the context and concept of this book will help dispel that nonsense. I appreciate Dr. Bell's honoring of the ministry of helps, however. It has done much to elevate the understanding of and the appreciation of how the ministry of helps is so vital to the church, but it is not an either/or proposition as the context clearly shows.

Administrations

Administrations/governments – to steer, pilotage, directorship. Likely these people function as administrators (motivationally). They are ones who help keep the ministry on track. They are specially anointed for the task and are of great benefit to the senior leadership as they often handle the practical and mundane affairs of the church that just have to be done. Often behind the scenes, these men and women are a great blessing to the leaders of the congregation.

As they learn to function administratively in the natural realm, Holy Spirit would also teach them to function in the realm of the Spirit and learn to administrate by the Spirit. They have to maintain a degree of sensitivity to the Holy Spirit, especially when the Local Apostle gives directives for significant changes and often does this with little warning. They must embrace the grace to handle those kinds of changes.

Tongues & Interpretation of Tongues

This particular appointment in the local church is one few have considered. It involves the coordination of two distinctive spiritual operations:

- Varieties of tongues – one who ministers in various languages.
- Interpretation of tongues – one who interprets the languages ministered.

The general purpose of tongues and interpretation of tongues is to unveil mysteries [32]. Likely this appointment involves ministry to both individuals and to the body revealing the will of God, mysteries, and insights. My wife and I have functioned in this capacity in several churches over the years. Unfortunately, the ministry of tongues and interpretation has been neglected in the church to a significant degree. A principle of honor is: What you honor, you have the benefit of. As the body of Christ, we have not honored this working of the Spirit in our midst and therefore do not have the benefit of it. The aspect of tongues being a sign to unbelievers[33] has been lost to the church. In the 1950s - 1960s, Rev. and Mrs. J. R. Goodwin, pastors of First Assembly of God in Pasadena, Texas, functioned fluently in this ministry in their local church. Several of their spiritual sons and daughters have continued to function similarly as well, long after the Goodwin's passing. As a former pastor of mine was one of their spiritual kids, I, no doubt, am a recipient of this supernatural working in my life.

Although verse 28 of 1 Corinthians does not explicitly mention "interpretation of tongues" as one of the appointments

---

[32] 1 Corinthians 14:2, 5

[33] Therefore tongues are for a sign, not to those who believe but to unbelievers; but prophesying is not for unbelievers but for those who believe. 1 Corinthians 14:22

in the local body, two verses later he brings the two (tongues and interpretation) back together.

> ²⁸And God has appointed these in the church: first apostles, second prophets, third teachers, after that miracles, then gifts of healings, helps, administrations, varieties of tongues. ²⁹Are all apostles? *Are* all prophets? *Are* all teachers? *Are* all workers of miracles? ³⁰Do all have gifts of healings? Do all speak with tongues? Do all interpret? 1 Corinthians 12:28-30

As Paul gave extensive instruction in 1 Corinthians 14 concerning the operation of tongues, interpretation of tongues, and prophecy, it seems no stretch to assume that the ministry of interpretation of tongues is as much an appointment by God in the local church as is the apostle, prophet, or teacher. We know from 1 Corinthians 14 that Paul always considered them companion operations.

Another aspect of these ministry twins is in the area of intercession. From studying 1 Corinthians 13-14, we know that tongues can be of men or of angels and as such they are, in essence, the trumpet blasts that give instruction to the angels in matters of war, just as trumpets were used in the Old Testament battles to direct the armies in conducting battle (See Numbers

10). Often the tongues and interpretation of tongues will function along with the prophetic office in bringing direction to the church. Again, we do not have the benefit of these operations in our churches because we have not honored them, or we have put them away in a closet somewhere hoping they will not cause trouble.

The following chart gives a summary of the functions of these appointments in the local church.

Appointment	Function
Apostle	Directional/Correctional
Prophet	Directional
Teacher	Instructional
Workers of Miracles	Evangelistic
Gifts of Healings	Evangelistic
Helps	Practical
Administration/Governments	Practical
Tongues	Intercessory
Interpretation of Tongues	Intercessory/Inspirational

Summary

\	APPOINTMENTS
Giver	God
Gift	Apostles, Prophets, Teachers, Workers of Miracles, Gifts of Healings, Helps, Governments, Tongues, Interpretation of Tongues
Giftee	Select Individuals in the body
Scope	The Local Body of Christ
Purpose	Equip the saints for the work of the ministry on a local level

SECTION 4

Apostles

As mentioned earlier, three different types of apostles can be clearly delineated in scripture. Scripture bears this out quite readily. Other applications of the apostolic gift exist, but will not be discussed at this time. The term "apostle" refers to a "delegated authority," "sent forth one," i.e. "a captain of a ship." Most of us have heard the definition "sent one," but most have not understood the meaning as including a "delegated authority." The man we know as Paul the Apostle was certainly sent, but it was within that "sending" that he operated as the delegated authority in whatever area he was sent to.

The Aramaic translation of the New Testament by Dr. James Murdock uses the term *"legate"* instead of the term apostle. This term would have been familiar to those living in the first century as a legate was a governor or general of a Roman province. As an example, King Herod was a legate. A legate was the primary authority over that area, and it was his particular responsibility to bring the culture and life of the country he served to bear in the province in his responsibility. It is this picture that I believe Dr. Murdock wanted us to grasp. Just as Jesus instructed his followers to "go and make disciples of every nation," [34] it was this picture that Jesus had in mind. When the Roman army invaded a people group, they intended that new domain to reflect Rome fully, and they were not satisfied until that was accomplished. Douglas Wilson, the author of *Heaven Misplaced*, describes it in this manner:

> Earth now has a new capital city— heaven— and we are called to learn how to live in terms of this. And as we learn, we are to teach. "For our conversation [lit., citizenship] is in heaven; from whence also we look for the Saviour, the Lord Jesus Christ: Who shall change our vile body, that it may be fashioned like unto his glorious body, according to the working whereby he is able even to subdue all things unto himself." (Phil. 3: 20– 21) As N.T. Wright notes, Caesar Augustus established the Roman colony of Philippi after the battle of Philippi in 42 B.C. and the battle of Actium in 31 B.C. He did this by settling his veterans there,

---

[34] Matthew 28:19

many of whom were Roman citizens. This is the backdrop for Paul's comment to the church that was located at this same Philippi. The Roman citizens of Philippi were there as Roman colonists, intended to extend the range and force of Roman influence throughout the Mediterranean world. They were not there in order for them to leave Philippi to come back to Rome for retirement.[35]

Apostles are to spearhead this conversion of the society to reflect that which Jesus taught us in Matthew 6:10 when he taught us to pray.

Your kingdom come. Your will be done on earth as *it is* in heaven.

The necessity of all the parts of the body functioning together becomes even more evident as we understand the task before us. We need the Ascension Gifts working with the Appointments in the body. We need the individual members understanding their foundational giftings so they can maximize their time and purpose upon the earth.

---

[35] Wilson, Douglas. Heaven Misplaced: Christ's Kingdom on Earth (Kindle Locations 213-221). Canon Press. Kindle Edition.

Though I hear many declare how dark it seems to be getting in the earth, I am reminded how every morning, just before the breaking of day, the night seems darker—it is merely a preparation for the coming Glory of the Lord as it breaks forth upon us!

> Arise, shine; For your light has come! And the glory of the LORD is risen upon you. ² For behold, the darkness shall cover the earth, and deep darkness the people; but the LORD will arise over you, and His glory will be seen upon you. ³ The Gentiles shall come to your light, and kings to the brightness of your rising. Isaiah 60:1-3

As we see in both 1 Corinthians 12:8 and Ephesians 4:11 the hierarchy was apostles, then prophets. They work together, but the apostle was the chief office. It was never about titles, but about servanthood and responsibility. In the New Testament writings of Paul, Peter, and John, the Apostle is always the first office mentioned, then the prophet.

Nearly equal coverage was given both offices:

Apostle or apostles 69 times in NKJV

Prophet or prophets 63 times in NKJV

The apostles and prophets are cornerstone offices in the body of Christ:

> ²⁰ having been built on the foundation of the apostles and prophets, Jesus Christ Himself being the chief cornerstone, ²¹ in whom the whole building, being fitted together, grows into a holy temple in the Lord. Ephesians 2:20-21

As "cornerstone" offices they help secure the foundation that the church is built upon. They are foundational offices according to the New Testament writings, not an afterthought or a relic of history. They are needed today as much as they were in the first century!

Apostles & Prophets are recipients of reserved revelation:

> ...how that by revelation He (God) made known to me the mystery (as I have briefly written already, ⁴ by which, when you read, you may understand my knowledge in the mystery of Christ), ⁵which in other ages was not made known to the sons of men, as it has now been revealed by the Spirit to His holy apostles and prophets. Ephesians 3:5

We, as the body of Christ, need what the apostles and prophets bring to the table. They help bring secure direction which is sorely needed in the church to this day. We need the revelation they can bring, and because revelation is progressive, and we have lacked much of the revelation that is available, we have been unable to accomplish what we, as the body of Christ, should have in establishing the Kingdom of God upon the earth and discipling nations (Matthew 28:19). Apostles are frontrunners and forerunners as are the prophets. We need the grace they bring. We cannot embrace a grace that we are not willing to partake of. That too must change!

Types of Apostles

International Apostles (Ephesians 4)

Paul was the apostle to the Gentiles throughout the world. This was an international anointing with subsequent grace for the ministry to which he was called. Let us take a look:

> ⁴⁶Then Paul and Barnabas grew bold and said, "It was necessary that the word of God should be spoken to you (Jews) first; but since you reject it, and judge yourselves unworthy of everlasting life, behold, we

> turn to the Gentiles. ⁴⁷For so the Lord had commanded us: 'I HAVE SET YOU AS A LIGHT TO THE GENTILES, THAT YOU SHOULD BE FOR SALVATION TO THE ENDS OF THE EARTH[36].'" ⁴⁸Now when the Gentiles heard this, they were glad and glorified the word of the Lord. And as many as had been appointed to eternal life believed. Acts 13:46-48

Apostles are notorious for knowing their place and their function in the body of Christ. Paul was indeed no exception. He knew that the Jews would be given the first opportunity to respond to the revelation of Jesus as the Messiah, but he also knew that if they rejected the offer, then the Gentiles would be next in line. Acts 13 records when this happened as the Jews in Antioch rejected the opportunity to receive the Messiah.

Peter, on the other hand, had as his primary focus ministry to the Jews worldwide. Paul describes their ministry in this passage:

> But on the contrary, when they saw that the gospel for the uncircumcised had been committed to me, as *the gospel* for the circumcised *was* to Peter ⁸(for He who worked effectively in Peter for the apostleship to the

---
[36] Isaiah 49:6

circumcised also worked effectively in me toward the Gentiles). Galatians 2:7-8

Peter, like Paul, had a corresponding grace for his ministry. The epistles of both men and the book of Acts are replete with their acknowledgment that they knew they were called as apostles and they understood the scope of their ministry.

We see in Acts 14:21-23 a few of the things that were common to apostles:

- Establish the Gospel in unreached areas
- Oversee the regional apostles & hence the churches in their care
- Ordain apostles and others
- Set decrees
- Confirm
- Exhort

Regional Apostles (Ephesians 4)

A reading of 1 & 2 Timothy reveals that Timothy (Paul's "son" in the faith[37]) was actually the apostle to the churches in the region of Ephesus. He may also have functioned as the local

---

[37] Philippians 2:22

apostle over the main church at Ephesus, but we know that he was charged with overseeing the churches around Ephesus. This was a regional apostolic anointing. Paul records in 1 Timothy 1 that he had sent Timothy to straighten out errors in teaching that had been propagated among the churches in the region of Ephesus. Ephesus was not merely a city or town, but also a region encompassing other towns and villages. Due to church planting, more than one church existed in the vicinity. However, they were without oversight until Timothy was sent to take on the responsibility and deal with some doctrinal issues among these churches. Unlike Paul, his geographic authority was limited to the region around Ephesus, whereas Paul could minister with corresponding authority wherever he was found himself as long as he focused on ministry to the Gentiles. As he did so, his ministry demonstrated much fruit. This is not to say that he had no authority to minister to the Jews, but rather that he had a specific authority to minister to the Gentiles.

Titus also had a regional apostolic anointing. His geographic placement was to the churches on the Isle of Crete. Paul writes to him:

> [4]To Titus, a true son in *our* common faith: Grace, mercy, *and* peace from God the Father and the Lord Jesus Christ our Savior. [5]For this reason I left you in

Crete, that you should set in order the things that are lacking, and appoint elders in every city as I commanded you. Titus 1:4-5

Crete was an island in the Mediterranean that had been evangelized, and churches apparently had been planted in every city. It is probable that this evangelism occurred due to conversions of Cretans on the Day of Pentecost (See Acts 2:11). However, the Cretans lacked in robust and mature leadership, so Titus was sent by Paul to (1) "set in order the things that are lacking," and (2) "appoint elders in every city." Titus did not have an easy task, for Paul, a few verses later, describes both their reputation and how to deal with the Cretans in this passage:

> [12]One of them, a prophet of their own, said, "Cretans *are* always liars, evil beasts, lazy gluttons." [13]This testimony is true. Therefore rebuke them sharply, that they may be sound in the faith. Titus 1:12-13

In the surrounding verses, Paul outlines some of the issues to be dealt with which would require a robust and steady hand. Titus was apparently up to the task since Paul had assigned it to him, confident in his ability to accomplish the goals given to him.

In our present day, we also find Regional Apostles who oversee the work of various churches and ministries. Often these

Regional Apostles were the founders of these works that they turned over to others to lead but retained a degree of apostolic oversight. This is a model we need to further develop in this day and to utilize in church planting efforts. We have often seen churches start that were never planted following the model found in the book of Acts model. Others have adequately covered that subject so we will not do so here. Another strength of the Regional Apostle is that they, because of their geographic proximity to the churches under their care, can maintain a more intimate relationship with those churches. If the senior leadership needs intervention or support, they are close enough to be able to provide it. This is difficult if they are too spread out geographically. Titus' situation of overseeing the churches on the Island of Crete presents a good model.

Another of the duties of the Regional (and International) Apostolic Offices was to settle disputes. Luke records for us:

Settle disputes

> When therefore Paul and Barnabas had no small dissension and disputation with them, they determined that Paul and Barnabas, and certain others of them, should go up to Jerusalem unto the apostles and elders about this question. Acts 15:2

As discussed in another part of this book, the apostles collectively came up with directives for the believers and settled for them how they should respond to the particular error that was trying to creep into that church.

Keep doctrine on track

> As I urged you when I went into Macedonia—remain in Ephesus that you may charge some that they teach no other doctrine. 1Timothy 1:3

Set in order the things that are lacking

> For this reason, I left you in Crete, that you should set in order the things that are lacking, and appoint elders in every city as I commanded you—Titus 1:5

> But if anyone is hungry, let him eat at home, lest you come together for judgment. And the rest I will set in order when I come. 1 Corinthians 11:34

Ordain Elders

> For this reason, I left you in Crete, that you should set in order the things that are lacking, and appoint elders in every city as I commanded you—Titus 1:5

Therefore I remind you to stir up the gift of God which is in you through the laying on of my hands. 2 Timothy 1:6

Make Disciples

You, therefore, my son, be strong in the grace that is in Christ Jesus. 2 Timothy 2:1

(See all of 2 Timothy)

Local Apostles (1 Corinthians 12)

James (the author of James; Jacobus[38] is his real name), the half-brother of Jesus, functioned differently than Titus or Timothy. He was a Local Apostle (1 Corinthians 12:28[39]) to the church in Jerusalem. He was the primary one in the local church in Jerusalem. Because Jerusalem was the center of the Christian world at that time, James also functioned as the convening (or presiding) apostle when councils convened at Jerusalem. He was

---

[38] Strong. G2385. *Jacobus.*

[39] 1 Corinthians 12:28 And God has appointed these in the church: first apostles, second prophets, third teachers, after that miracles, then gifts of healings, helps, administrations, varieties of tongues.

in charge because it was held in his place of authority (see Acts 15).

Ephesians 4 tells us that each ministry gift has a corresponding grace that needs to be partaken of by the individual believers. James may also have been an apostle in the sense of Ephesians 4, but a study of the book of Acts will show that he was the presiding elder of the Jerusalem church. This position is in keeping with 1 Corinthians 12:28 where Paul records that God has set in the church (local) first of all apostles, secondarily prophets, thirdly teachers, etc. This is exemplified in Acts as it tells us that working with James were various prophets and teachers (Acts 12:17; 15:13; 21:18).

They are the senior leadership position in a local body; essentially they are the CEO/chief executive officer. They oversee the ministries emanating from the local body of believers. The term Bishop (or Overseer) could also apply as they "oversee" the local body, and it is synonymous with the local apostolic office. Remember that the church in Jerusalem was quite large. Our present model of a pastor-centric leadership would not work well in Jerusalem, for the scope of responsibilities would be far beyond the abilities of one person to handle. According to Acts 20:17, 28, Philippians 1:1, these elders are also overseers. The example of the church in Jerusalem had the Local Apostle as the chief among the elders (See Acts 15).

In Acts 20:28 we read:

> Therefore take heed to yourselves and to all the flock, among which the Holy Spirit has made you **overseers**, to shepherd the church of God which He purchased with His own blood. (Emphasis mine)

This is the only passage that refers to the role of a shepherd (as a tender-feeder) concerning the local church. Yet nowhere in the New Testament do we find anyone referred to as a pastor or shepherd. The terms are synonymous. The pastor as a senior leader has no scriptural precedent. No example exists in the New Testament. The Local Apostle is the man or woman set in charge over the house. I will cover this more thoroughly when we begin discussing "teaching pastors." Some of the duties listed concerning international and regional apostles also apply to the local apostolic office, such as:

- Keeping doctrine on track (1 Tim 1:3)
- Setting in order the things that are lacking (Titus 1:5)
- Ordaining elders (Titus 1:5)

Unfortunately, even major Pentecostal denominations have missed the point when it comes to understanding the apostolic office and functions. In August 2001, the Assemblies of God headquartered in Springfield, Missouri issued a position paper regarding apostles and prophets. Here is a portion of their conclusions on the matter:

> *Since the New Testament does not provide guidance for the appointment of future apostles, such contemporary offices are not essential to the health and growth of the church, nor its apostolic nature.*[40]

Concerning prophets, they concluded:

> *The New Testament does not make provisions for establishing the prophet in a hierarchical governing structure of the church; in fact, the content of prophecy itself should always be tested by and responsible to the superior authority of Scripture.*[41]

Ironically, the same basis they used for the apostolic could be noted for their view of the pastoral, which they do embrace using

---

[40] http://ag.org/top/Beliefs/Position_Papers/pp_downloads/pp_4195_apostles_prophets.pdf (10)

[41] http://ag.org/top/Beliefs/Position_Papers/pp_downloads/pp_4195_apostles_prophets.pdf (10)

the five-fold paradigm. What scriptural guidance exists for the appointment of future pastors?

The International Church of the Foursquare Gospel has been more open to recognition of the apostolic-centered paradigm of church government. Though I know of no official position papers issued by them, I have witnessed the embrace of the apostolic paradigm at various levels within the Foursquare movement, a movement which has a far more significant impact overseas than it has within the boundaries of the United States.

The International Pentecostal Holiness Church, in a position paper entitled: "Apostolic Biblical Statement and Practical Guidelines" had this to say about apostles:

> *We conclude there are persons identified as "apostles" in the New Testament at this functional level. Also, at this level, it is reasonable to believe the ministry gift of the apostle has always existed in the Lord's church and continues to this day.*[42]

The position paper goes on to provide good teaching on what they termed "functional apostles."

---

[42] http://iphc.org/position-papers/ Apostolic Position Papers (9)

Other Earmarks of the Apostle

These earmarks are not restricted to any level of the apostolic but need to be reviewed when looking at the apostolic office. These earmarks were experienced by Paul, Peter and many of the others.

- Persecutions (Acts 13:50; 2 Corinthians 12:10; 2 Timothy 3:11)
- Trials (Acts 20:19-Paul)
- Tribulations (Acts 20:23; 2 Corinthians 6:4)

However, regardless of the trials, tribulations, and persecutions, Paul describes how they only seemed to increase the level of Glory operating in his life:

> [17]For our light affliction, which is but for a moment, is working for us a far more exceeding *and* eternal weight of glory, [18]while we do not look at the things which are seen, but at the things which are not seen. For the things which are seen *are* temporary, but the things which are not seen *are* eternal. 2 Corinthians 4:17-18

Four Aspects of Apostolic Authority

1. Ranks of Apostleship

James was apparently the Chief Apostle at Jerusalem as well as the Local Apostle over the believers in that city. This was a dual role as Jerusalem was the international headquarters of the church at that time.

Paul indicates the same concept of chief apostles in 2 Corinthians 11:5; 12:11 as well as lesser apostles in 1 Corinthians 15:9.

The scriptural distinction between Ephesians 4 (Ascension Gift) Apostleship and 1 Corinthians 12:28 Apostleship is the scope of ministry and the subsequent realm of authority, as we have been discussing.

2. Reach of Authority

Each apostle is given a specific sphere of authority (2 Corinthians 10:13-16).

International

- Paul's sphere - the Gentile world (Romans 11:13)
- Peter's sphere - the Jewish world (Galatians 2:8)

Regional

- Titus had the Island of Crete (Titus 1:4-5)
- Timothy had the churches of Ephesus (1 Timothy 1:2-3)

Local

- James – apostle of the Jerusalem church (Galatians 1:19, 1 Corinthians 15:7, Acts 21:18)

3. *Relational Authority*

"Relationship, not hierarchy, is the basis of spiritual authority." - Dick Iverson

You are not in authority unless you are under authority (Luke 7:8)

An apostle is not necessarily an apostle to all. Some are under the sphere of authority of another. See I Corinthians 9:2, where Paul was in oversight of Timothy, Titus, and others.

4. *Regional Authority*

"Regional" or "Territorial" apostleship.

Timothy and Titus exhibit this. Paul's ministry took him to Palestine, Syria, Cyprus, Asia Minor, Macedonia, Greece, and Rome as well as Illyricum and Spain. (Romans 15:19-24). Peter traveled to Babylon (modern Iraq) (I Peter 5:13).

The historian Eusebius says that the "inhabited world" was divided into zones of influence among the apostles: Thomas in the region of the Parthians, John in Asia, Peter in Pontus and Rome, Andrew in Scythia (The Christian Centuries, J. Danielou, p. 39)

A further breakdown of this is the Local Apostle over a local body as in 1 Corinthians 12:28.

Coupled with this geographic understanding is the concept of *metrons*. *Metron* means "measure" or "degree." It refers to the measure of rule one possesses.

> [13]But we will not boast of things without *our* **measure**, but according to the **measure** of the rule which God hath distributed to us, a **measure** to reach even unto you. [14]For we stretch not ourselves beyond *our measure*, as though we reached not unto you: for we are come as far as to you also in *preaching* the gospel of Christ: [15]not boasting of things without *our* **measure**, *that is,* of other men's labors; but having

hope, when your faith is increased, that we shall be enlarged by you according to our rule abundantly, ¹⁶to preach the gospel in the *regions* beyond you, *and* not to boast in another man's line of things made ready to our hand. 2 Corinthians 10:13-16 (emphasis mine)

Paul understood the concept of "specific" authority. He possessed a specific authority to share the Gospel with the Gentiles, regardless of their pagan background, while Peter focused on the Jews. Although Peter ministered to the Gentiles, his focus was always on ministry to the Jews to see them embrace the Messiah.

In my own life, I possess a specific authority in certain states within the United States. In the states in which I do not possess a specific authority, I defer to those individuals who do possess specific authority in those places. Paul pointed out that he did not want to minister where someone else had already ministered. No shortage of unbelievers existed at that time, nor does it now. As a matter of fact, some records indicate that around 100 A.D. you could find one believer for every 360 people (1:360), now that number worldwide is closer to one believer for every seven

(1:7)⁴³—a massive increase in the number of believers on the planet.

Ministering Out of the Office

Within the apostolic office exists a strength that does not exist in the other offices. Apostles are to create sons, and an aspect of that fathering dimension requires a strength out of which they must operate. As I was writing along these lines, I heard Holy Spirit say, "I want a new level of that [apostolic fathering] existing in the earth. I want sons created. They should be forerunners in sonship and should bring others along with them."

When apostles prophesy, a degree of strength is often exhibited that is not present in any of the other offices or placements. When an apostle prophesies, they need to be cognizant of doing so out of the strength of the apostolic office to which they are called -- this is true whether they are Ascension Gift apostles, or 1 Corinthians 12:28 (Placement) apostles.

When they teach, the same scenario occurs. One who is an apostle may often function as a teacher, for example, and can

---

[43] Finishing the Task (544) - Ralph D. Winter and Bruce A. Koch - www.frontierventures.org.

operate out of the anointing of a teacher, but more significant results may occur if they operate out of the apostolic and tap into the teacher anointing. They must teach out of the apostolic anointing rather than the teaching anointing, which they can access. The teaching drives into the hearts of the people, surpassing a merely mental level, but when they teach from/out of the apostolic anointing, it can drive the truth and revelation even deeper into the hearts of the listeners. In every way, they should operate on a different level of strength than they would normally.

It is the same with the prophetic arena. Much has been said about prophetic declarations, but I believe a stronger dimension exists where an apostle can declare out of the apostolic office, rather than declaring "prophetically." Thus, I encourage those who are apostles to prophesy apostolically, not merely prophetically.

> You will also declare a thing, and it will be established for you; so light will shine on your ways. Job 22:28

A grace and unction specific to the apostolic office exist that is on a different plane than the other Ascension Gifts or placements. The specific strength of this office was demonstrated rather vividly when the apostle Peter confronted Ananias and

Sapphira, who each immediately fell dead at his feet after lying to Holy Spirit. Peter was clear to point out that they had not lied to him, but more pointedly, they had lied to Holy Spirit.

The ability to declare and see it occur arises out of the apostolic office. The Old Testament parallel to the apostolic was often portrayed through the imagery of a king. A noticeable characteristic of kings is that they did not function by swinging a sword, but rather by wielding a scepter. Decrees were formalized via the wielding of the scepter by the king, and actions taken on behalf of the king were thus validated. We need to learn to wield the scepter of authority given to us as apostles rather than always trying to "duke it out" with various principalities of darkness or that one using an older paradigm of warfare. Apostles recognize that they do not have to go into battle situations swinging swords, as we were taught so many years in the spiritual warfare movement, but rather that much more will be accomplished when we learn to wield the scepter of authority we have been granted in the realms in for which it was granted.

When they are in the evangelistic mode, again the apostle carries a strength that is not as prevalent in the other offices. Signs and wonders should be commonplace for them. We saw that they were commonplace in the life of Paul and should expect the same, but it requires stepping into the authority of that office to see it demonstrated.

Recently, the opportunity arose to ordain a young man in the ministry. As hands were laid upon him and his wife, angels began to manifest, and the spirit of prophecy was released in the place we were meeting. Other manifestations of the glory of the Lord were evident that day. When room is given to the prophetic dimension, the prophetic dimension will accommodate and do wondrous things. If you have not seen much in the way of supernatural manifestations, then perhaps you should evaluate whether you are making room for it.

Apostles need to function under the mantle of their office. As we learn to tap into the supernatural arena and strength of the apostolic office, we will see things shift in unlimited ways in the church and in the earth. Much is to be done, but it must be done with the strength of the equipment Holy Spirit has given us.

Apostolic Functions

When teaching on the apostolic, I discovered the following functions discussed in the New Testament. I will lay them out and discuss them briefly as they need it.

Apostles Bring Order

> But if anyone is hungry, let him eat at home, lest you come together for judgment. And the rest **I will set in order** when I come. 1Corinthians 11:34

The Corinthian believers were abusing The Lord's Supper by irreverence toward it. Paul understood the potential problems this could cause and in fact and had already caused, saying some had died prematurely as a result. Apostles often see potential dangers and are used by God to warn the church before further damage is done.

In another passage, we have Paul bringing instruction to the same believers concerning the proper uses of prophecy, tongues, and interpretation of tongues. Much of his first letter to the Corinthians was to set things in order. In chapter 14 we read:

> Let all things be done decently and in order. 1Corinthians 14:40

We know from other readings that Titus was charged with setting things in order over the churches on the island of Crete (Titus 1:5).

By the same token, apostles strongly dislike disorder. When they see it, something inside them wants to rise up and bring correction. They dislike seeing the manifestations of the Spirit abused or misused, and they dislike seeing others bring harm to the body. They want life flowing in the body of Christ at every level, not death!

Apostles Settle Doctrinal Disputes

In Acts 15:1-2, 6, we have one of the most distinctive examples of the apostles, along with the other elders, settling a doctrinal dispute. Acts 15:1 tells us what it was:

> And certain *men* came down from Judea and taught the brethren, "Unless you are circumcised according to the custom of Moses, you cannot be saved."

The believers then did not have the letter to the Hebrews that we do possess to see how clearly and completely Jesus' sacrifice fulfilled and eliminated the continuing need for circumcision and animal sacrifices. In their day, that system was winding down and would be annihilated entirely once the temple was destroyed (which occurred in 70 A.D). As the council gathered to make a determination on this matter, Peter arose and gave clarity to the question at hand. Out of this council came their determination which brings us to another function of the apostolic.

Apostles Make Decrees

In the last half of chapter 15, we find the council formulating a letter for Paul and Barnabas to carry with them back to Antioch. Although this was not shouted from the housetops like we tend to think of decrees being proclaimed, their response to the error being taught was to bring forth a summary for the believers to follow, which they presented to the believers in Antioch upon their return. The reasoned conclusion of that apostolic council comes out in the brief contents of the letter of which we have record:

> For it seemed good to the Holy Spirit, and to us, to lay upon you no greater burden than these necessary things: that you abstain from things offered to idols, from blood, from things strangled, and from sexual immorality. If you keep yourselves from these, you will do well. Farewell. Acts 15:28-29

In their collective wisdom, they simplified the Gospel from the Jewish and particularly of the Pharisaical influence that was trying to take hold of the early church. Thank God for reasoned solutions!

Apostles Set Deacons & Elders in Place

In Acts 6, we see the first example of the apostles and elders setting others in places of responsibility and authority. This is where the six men of good report, full of the Holy Spirit and wisdom,[44] were set in place as deacons. Also, in Acts 14:23, we read:

> So when they (Paul and Barnabas) had appointed elders in every church and prayed with fasting, they commended them to the Lord in whom they had believed.

Apostles Impart Giftings

Over the years, I have heard much debate on whether "gifts" could be imparted. Apparently, Paul thought so and said just that in Romans 1:11:

> For I long to see you, that I may impart to you some spiritual gift (*charisma*) so that you may be established.

---

[44] Acts 6:3

I have a limited understanding of this concept, however, from the next two passages, it is clear that Paul (and possibly others), had laid hands upon Timothy, and he received something.

> Therefore I remind you to stir up the gift (*charisma*) of God which is in you through the laying on of my hands. 2 Timothy 1:6

> Do not neglect the gift (*charisma*) that is in you, which was given to you by prophecy with the laying on of the hands of the eldership. 1Timothy 4:14

The gift Paul is writing about is the Motivational/Foundational kind. Instead of being religious about it and saying, "Bless God, you cannot give someone a gift, only God can!" we should realize that it is through men and women that God gives a lot of things. God is not always going to reach over from Heaven and do a thing. Instead, He chooses to use us.

Obviously, you do not just go around laying your hands on people indiscriminately, but rather prayerfully and in response to the instruction of Holy Spirit. Paul implies as much in 1 Timothy 5:22:

> Do not lay hands on anyone hastily, nor share in other people's sins; keep yourself pure.

Is it possible that Paul, by the laying on of his hands, imparted to Timothy part of his own perceiver/teacher motivation to strengthen the motivational gifting that was already present in Timothy?

Apostles Delegate Authority

A further function of the apostolic office (Ascension or Appointment) is to delegate to sub-apostolic leadership. Paul apparently did this concerning Timothy[45] and Titus,[46] and the Jerusalem church did it with Paul and Silas[47] and others[48].

Apostles Establish

Apostles establish churches, ministries, etc. The book of Acts is replete with the works of the apostles in establishing the church, believers, ministries, and more. In fact, some Bibles refer to Acts as "the Acts of the Apostles," while others call it "the Acts of the Holy Spirit." In either case, what started out with a small number in the upper room now numbers in the billions upon the earth!

---

[45] 1 Timothy 1
[46] Titus 1:5
[47] Acts 13:2
[48] Acts 6:6

Apostles Make commands

Peter in Acts 10:48, commands the new believers to be baptized in the name of the Lord. The Jerusalem Council in Acts 15:22-29 issued a short series of decrees as we studied earlier, and Paul, in 1 Thessalonians 4:2, alludes to commands he had earlier given the believers in Thessalonica. As Americans, we dislike being commanded to do anything. After all, we are proud of our American Revolution. We are still rebelling against those in authority over us to this day. Maybe that is part of the problem.

Other Functions

In my studies of the apostolic, I also noted a few other things.

- **Apostles may function in an office to which they are not explicitly called** (i.e., they perform the role).
    - Timothy instructed to do the work of an evangelist although he was a regional/local apostle (2 Timothy 4:5).
    - Paul was an apostle, prophet, teacher, and evangelist.
- **Apostles are likely to operate in all nine manifestations of the Spirit as needed.** Paul saw signs and wonders, raised people from the dead, ministered in

gifts of healings, operated in the discerning of spirits, word of knowledge, and word of wisdom. He spoke in tongues and prophesied (and also operated in the gift of faith as needed). He set the pattern for the apostolic office.

- **Apostles are often empowered to exert influence governmentally on an area within the realm of the spirit.** The apostolic office is a governing office and has the capacity to not only govern but to affect governments in the natural. Often when ministers feel an urge to run for political office, it may be because they sense a governmental calling, and interpret it to mean, "I've got to run for mayor!" or whatever office is available. They are mistaking running for office as the governmental aspect that is inherent in the apostolic office. If apostles fulfill the governing aspect correctly, they will indeed govern behind the scenes and have a significant influence on the natural and political realm by exercising their authority in the spirit realm.

- **Apostles are likely to have "come up through the ranks."** Paul and Silas had proven themselves as Prophets and Teachers when they were elevated and sent forth as Apostles.

Apostolic Manifestations

1. Apostles May Attract Large Crowds

The supernatural anointing upon an apostle will attract attention, and at times, large crowds. Paul dealt with both large crowds and home churches.

2. Apostles Possess a Supernatural Spirit of Revelation

Paul and Peter experienced visions, words of knowledge, and trances. He operated in the discerning of spirits and prophecy. (2 Corinthians 12:1-7; I Corinthians 11:23; Acts 10:9-22; 18:9-10; Acts 10:19,20; 16:16; 1 Timothy 1:18; 2 Timothy 1:6.)

3. Apostles Exercise Supernatural Command Over Sickness

We find a record of Peter and John (Acts 3:1) exercising supernatural command over sickness when they minister to the lame man at the Beautiful Gate. Peter heals the bedridden man (Acts 9:32-35), resulting in a massive evangelistic sweep in the town of Lydda.

Paul & Barnabas operated in signs and wonders (Acts 14:3; 14:6-10), and we also read where handkerchiefs were used to impart healing that Paul had anointed (Acts 19:11-12). Earlier in Acts, Peter's shadow was all it took to bring healing to people (Acts 5:15-16), and Paul records signs, wonders, and mighty deeds being performed in 2 Corinthians 12:20.

4. Apostles Exercise Supernatural Power Over Demons

The apostles exercised dramatic power over demons. (Acts 5:6; 8:7; 16:16-18; 19:12). All believers have authority over demons, but I dare say most of us do not recognize, nor operate within, that level of authority, as did Paul, Peter, and the others we read of in the New Testament. We all should, but simply put, we all do not.

6. Apostles Release Supernatural Power Against Wickedness

We see in Acts 5 that Peter was not going to play around with wickedness. When confronted with Ananias and his lying to the Holy Spirit, he exercised his authority. It is likely he took Jesus' words in John 20:23[49] to heart as death was released first upon Ananias, and, three hours later upon his wife, Sapphira. Luke records the results of that event:

---

[49] If you forgive the sins of any, they are forgiven them; if you retain the sins of any, they are retained. John 20:23

So great fear came upon all the church and upon all who heard these things. And through the hands of the apostles, many signs and wonders were done among the people. And they were all with one accord in Solomon's Porch. Acts 5:11-12

Peter protected the unity possessed by the early believers by not allowing the leaven of the sin of Ananias and Sapphira to go unchecked. We could learn a few lessons from this as well. (I discuss this more in Section 2.)

In Acts 13:8-11 we find Paul pronouncing judgment on Elymas, the sorcerer who goes blind for a season. The degree of authority Peter and Paul walked indirectly corresponds to their walk of holiness and their intolerance for sin or wickedness. Because they had nothing in common with the enemy, they had absolute power over the enemy, as did Jesus[50].

7. Apostles Manifest Supernatural Power to Raise the Dead

Paul, on two occasions that are recorded, raised the dead. Dorcas in Acts 9:36-42, and the young man who fell asleep and fell out of the window from the third floor (Acts 20:9-11).

---

[50] John 14:30

Raising the dead is to be on our *Curriculum Vitae* according to the instructions of Jesus in Matthew:

> Heal the sick, cleanse the lepers, **raise the dead**, cast out demons. Freely you have received, freely give. Matthew 10:8 (emphasis mine)

Speaking of the disciples and leaders of the early church, I recall years ago reading the following statement by (Phillips):

> *"Perhaps if we believed what they believed, we could achieve what they achieved."*

This is quite a statement for us to consider. We have more means to publicize the Gospel than ever before, but the question is, are we maximizing those means?

Other Earmarks of the Apostle

Although it is not our favorite subject, we must also look at a few other aspects that were earmarks of the apostle. These include being persecutions, trials, and tribulations. Following the Day of Pentecost, the church had a season of time where they were able to evangelize throughout Israel. However, in Acts 5, beginning at verse 17, we read of the start of the persecution of the church by the Jews. The Roman occupiers were not involved in this persecution, which lasted for a period of time. It is marked by the stoning of Stephen at its beginning and the later imprisonment of the apostles who were released from prison by an angel. The apostles, Peter among them, were found teaching and preaching Jesus the next day, and Peter gave a scathing rebuke to the Pharisees and Sadducees responsible for the imprisonment. The last verse of the chapter summarizes the impact of this first round of persecution:

> And daily in the temple, and in every house, they did not cease teaching and preaching Jesus as the Christ.
> Acts 5:42

Paul was imprisoned multiple times, which ultimately worked for our benefit, for it was from prison that Paul wrote most of his epistles to the churches. Around AD 67, under the Roman emperor Nero, persecution came upon the church in a whole new fashion and ferocity. During this time Peter, Paul, and many others were martyred. The destruction of the temple in AD 70 put an end to the persecution for a time, but it was not for nearly 200 years that it finally ceased. We have indications of these persecutions in Acts 13:50, 2 Corinthians 12:10, and 2 Timothy 3:11.

Another earmark to be noted were trials. In Acts 20:19, Paul mentions the trials he had undergone at the hands of the Jews. At this point in time, he was on his way to Jerusalem, and ultimately Rome, where he stated he did not know what awaited him, but he was not deterred in his going, although many of the believers tried to persuade him not to go. Paul knew via Holy Spirit that chains and tribulations awaited him.

In 2 Corinthians 6, we read Paul's resume' of ministry:

> [4] But in all things, we commend ourselves as ministers of God: in much patience, in tribulations, in needs, in distresses, [5] in stripes, in imprisonments, in tumults, in labors, in sleeplessness, in fastings.

A fuller version of his resume is found later in 2 Corinthians:

> Are they ministers of Christ?—I speak as a fool—I am more: in labors more abundant, in stripes above measure, in prisons more frequently, in deaths often. [24] From the Jews five times I received forty stripes minus one. [25] Three times I was beaten with rods; once I was stoned; three times I was shipwrecked; a night and a day I have been in the deep; [26] in journeys often, in perils of waters, in perils of robbers, in perils of my own countrymen, in perils of the Gentiles, in

perils in the city, in perils in the wilderness, in perils in the sea, in perils among false brethren; ²⁷ in weariness and toil, in sleeplessness often, in hunger and thirst, in fastings often, in cold and nakedness— ²⁸ besides the other things, what comes upon me daily: my deep concern for all the churches. 2 Corinthians 11:23-28

Yet Paul served faithfully, undeterred by these things, but rather making the most of the opportunities available. He gives a beautiful summary of his attitude in this passage:

Therefore I take pleasure in infirmities, in reproaches, in needs, in persecutions, in distresses, for Christ's sake. For when I am weak, then I am strong. 2 Corinthians 12:10

If we are found to have the calling of apostle, prophet, teacher, or any of these beautiful equippings for the body of Christ and His church, we must be willing to face the possibility that persecutions, trials, and tribulations may await us. Let us faithfully serve.

Prophets

The Prophetic Office & the Prophetic Appointment

When reviewing the prophetic office and the prophetic appointment, it is important to realize that prophets do not fit comfortably into any mold. In the Old Testament, you find loud prophets, quiet prophets, wordy prophets, and very reluctant prophets. You found prophets who spoke only of events impacting their direct sphere of influence, and others who spoke of things with a global impact. Why should we expect the New Testament to be any different in that regard?

In your everyday experience, you will find prophetically-oriented people who are not prophets, or you may find a prophet who has a mercy motivation (you will probably find them on their face in intercession). You will find prophets whose scope of ministry is a local church or ministry, prophets with a more extensive scope of ministry and still others with a national or an international reach. All of these we find examples of in the New Testament writings.

Along with understanding the scope of ministry, we must understand that just because a person prophesies, does not make him/her a prophet. Being prophetically oriented (as a motivational gift) does not make you a prophet, the call of God does! If you are a local prophet (set in a local church), it does not mean you have a regional or more extensive scope of authority. The prophet with the broader scope of authority may have authority to speak into the smaller scope, but not necessarily vice versa. As with any of the offices, we need to be sure to stay within our pay grade or scope of authority. Those having military experience understand that some things were not in your pay grade to do, and if they were not in your pay grade, you did not do them. It could get you in trouble.

The very definition of a prophet should give us an indication of these things. Prophets are forth-tellers meaning they speak forth an instruction, direction, and/or correction. They also are "fore-tellers" meaning their prophecies sometimes have a predictive element to them. We have Agabus the prophet predicting the famine in Acts 11:28. This predictive element has been greatly misunderstood throughout history, and when declaring that because a prophet's words did not come true, they, therefore, must be a false prophet. That is not a proper way of looking at it. If that definition or "litmus test" were used concerning Isaiah, Ezekiel, Daniel or others who prophesied events far into the future, then no one would be willing to step out and declare a prophetic word.

There is one aspect of the prophetic which is almost always present, which is the seer element. This means they often "see" into the realm of the spirit. We will not teach on the seer element for others have done a fine job of that already (Jim Goll is one name among many that come to mind). That seeing ability enables them to discern matters of direction, correction, and protection, not just for the body of Christ, but also the world at large. Sometimes the "seeing" is for the purpose of intercession where they will stand in the gap (to borrow a phrase from Ezekiel 22:30) and as they successfully intercede for the situation at hand, they are able to see it stayed, or at least mitigated in its impact.

We see in Acts 11:27-29 an example of this predictive element:

> [27] And in these days prophets came from Jerusalem to Antioch. [28] Then one of them, named Agabus, stood up and showed by the Spirit that there was going to be a great famine throughout all the world, which also happened in the days of Claudius Caesar. [29] Then the disciples, each according to his ability, determined to send relief to the brethren dwelling in Judea.

Apparently, this was not a "global" famine.if it had been sure, the believers in Antioch would have thought to provide relief for more than just the believers in Judea. In this case, the famine was concerning "their world," not necessarily for the entire planet. The prophetic foresight provided the ability to prepare for some very tough times for the believers at that era. History records a tremendous time of famine in the mid-first-century, bearing out what Agabus had seen and declared.

> *But the famine was too hard for all other passions, and it is destructive to nothing so much as to modesty . . . Insomuch that children pulled the very morsels that their fathers were eating out of their very mouths, and what was still more to be pitied, so did the mothers do as to their infants; and when those that were most dear were perishing under their hands, they were not ashamed to take from them the very last drops that might preserve their lives . . . but the seditious everywhere came upon them immediately, and snatched away from them what they had gotten from others; for when they saw any house shut up, this was to them a signal that the people within had gotten some food; whereupon they broke open the doors, and ran in and took pieces of what they were eating, almost up out of*

their very throats, and this by force; the old men, who held their food fast, were beaten; and if the women hid what they had within their hands, their hair was torn for so doing; nor was there any commiseration shown either to the aged or to the infants, but they lifted up children from the ground as they hung upon the morsels they had gotten, and shook them down upon the floor.

(The Wars of the Jews, 1998, V:X:3)

For those called to the regional or apostolic-prophetic office, the challenge for some will be to rise to the level where they are able to speak directly to kings and leaders of nations. Few have risen to this level of nation-impacting influence, although much more should arise. Because the prophetic cuts through much of the clutter in our atmospheres, they, along with the apostolic offices, are likely to be the recipients of much spiritual resistance. It is essential that they, in particular, keep their lives clean of all commonality with the enemy.

Another aspect of the prophetic ministry at all stages is how they are used to separate and release people into ministry. An example of that occurs in Acts 13.

> ¹Now there were in the church that was at Antioch certain prophets and teachers; as Barnabas, and Simeon that was called Niger, and Lucius of Cyrene, and Manaen, which had been brought up with Herod, the tetrarch, and Saul. ²As they ministered to the Lord, and fasted, the Holy Ghost said, Separate me Barnabas and Saul for the work whereunto I have called them. ³And when they had fasted and prayed and laid their hands on them, they sent them away. ⁴So they, being sent forth by the Holy Ghost, departed unto Seleucia; and from thence they sailed to Cyprus. Acts 13:1-4

and again

> ³²Now Judas and Silas, themselves being prophets also, exhorted and strengthened the brethren with many words. ³³And after they had stayed there for a time, they were sent back with greetings from the brethren to the apostles. Acts 15:32-33

> ¹⁰And as we stayed many days, a certain prophet named Agabus came down from Judea. ¹¹When he had come to us, he took Paul's belt, bound his own hands and feet, and said, "Thus says the Holy Spirit, 'So shall the Jews at Jerusalem bind the man who owns

> this belt, and deliver him into the hands of the Gentiles. Acts 21:10-11

A common thread of the prophetic is to propel others into ministry and to let them know what they see. As with Agabus' "seeing" a man bound hands and feet, their natural response was to hope this would not happen to Paul (the man in the vision). To Paul, however, this prophetic act was merely confirming to him what lay ahead in his future. Paul was no stranger to tough assignments, and he was not about to change that. He actually had to be somewhat blunt to the other apostles, prophets, and teachers and let them know that he would not be deterred in his mission.

The foundational building element of the prophetic needs to be mentioned here. Paul wrote:

> [19]Now, therefore, you are no longer strangers and foreigners, but fellow citizens with the saints and members of the household of God, [20] having been built on the foundation of the apostles and prophets, Jesus Christ Himself being the chief corner*stone,* [21] in whom the whole building, being fitted together, grows into a holy temple in the Lord, [22] in whom you also are being

built together for a dwelling place of God in the Spirit.
Ephesians 2:19-22

Both the apostolic and the prophetic offices carry with them a degree of foundation building not noted about the other offices. They want to see the church firmly built on a solid footing. The prophetic provides insight into potential trouble spots and is useful when identifying encroachments of the enemy into the church. What may seem harmless to everyone else will likely raise a flag to the prophets and apostles among us. In things others ignore, they will see the potential for destruction hidden inside. It is this ability to unveil the demonic and remove the covering of the occult that causes particular problems for the enemy. The fact that this apostolic and prophetic eye and voice has been virtually silenced for centuries as the church fell into the trap of being lulled to sleep by those who had no cutting edge voice. It is precisely what we need today to slice through the barrage of peripheral issues and deal with the roots of the problems that are impacting the church and subsequently impacting the world at large.

Any sin issue we see is the result of a failure at some level of the church. We are surrounded by what apostolic voice Floyd McClung refers to as false solutions. We need the prophetic eye to be brought to the forefront to cause the church to see the inherent problems and make the changes it needs to make. The prophetic will bring awareness, but when coupled with the apostolic strength and voice, it will be able to bring the Church out of darkness when the prophetic is released to operate as it should.

Ephesians 3:5 speaks of the mystery of Christ being unveiled through the ministry of the apostles and prophets:

> Which in other ages was not made known unto the sons of men, as it is now revealed unto his holy apostles and prophets by the Spirit; Ephesians 3:5

As the church, we must function via revelation. We have operated for centuries primarily on knowledge without many revelations. That method has served to dull the edge of the blade, so to speak, concerning our impact upon society. The degree of impact that the apostolic/prophetic combo has is yet to be seen in the strength required, but it shall in the coming days as men and women rise to their place in the body of Christ and declare "Thus says the Lord!"

Revelatory understandings are going to come forth that will put the body of Christ on a new level and operating in a new degree of strength that will cause the powers of Hell to tremble and bow. The church is arising!

One such understanding is the platform of prayer known as the Courts of Heaven. Understanding of this paradigm of prayer is only now being released into the body of Christ, and with it, a new level of effectiveness in prayer. The potential of this paradigm has yet to be tapped.

James notes an aspect of the prophetic that we do not usually want to talk about: persecution. We, in this century, have certainly not progressed past a time when men and women are persecuted for their faith. We are rarely shocked anymore by the reports of how extremists are persecuting believers around the globe. However, we must remember that this is not a new experience for the church. Tremendous persecution occurred against the early church in the first century. Paul, among many others, died at the hands of Emperor Nero during this time. James did point out that their example may have outlived their physical bodies, but it did not outlive them; they merely graduated to Heaven.

> Take, my brethren, the prophets, who have spoken in the name of the Lord, for an example of suffering affliction, and of patience. James 5:10

Earlier I spoke of the scope of the prophetic. Like the apostolic and the teacher, they each have a particular scope of authority. Some are local in their operations, others regional, and still others international in scope. We need the prophetic voice to see into the future and then for strategies to come forth to deal with what has been seen efficiently. Those with a local assignment as a prophet have the ability to speak prophetically to that local body. Those with a broader scope of service can speak to that arena as well as those local bodies within that area. Still, others, whose assignment is an even more extensive realm of influence, can speak into that realm as well as the realms under its jurisdiction.

Much of the unnecessary bickering and fighting over the centuries could have been avoided if we had given place to the prophetic voice and not written them off as kooks or weirdos. Being a prophet and being referred to as "crazy" or "madman" is nothing new. It has always been part and parcel of the office. (See 2 Kings 9:11)

Local Prophetic Function

> ...and God has set some in the church...secondarily prophets. 1 Corinthians 12:28

God has granted these individuals the specific authority to speak into the lives of the local body. They may not possess any authority to speak outside of that local body, but they indeed possess the authority to speak to them. Honoring this role will allow that body to be on the cutting edge of what God desires to do in that locale. These prophets may also serve as watchmen or gatekeepers to that church, and as such will also serve as intercessors. I have watched over the years as prophets have served local bodies with the God-ordained intent of keeping them on track. When they stopped being honored, the body often strayed from its purpose onto good things, but not necessarily things that were the design of God for that body. Good things are not always the best things for us. We must determine to never settle for the good when we are to have the best—the highest will of God for our lives, churches, and ministries.

Prophetic Manifestations

1. *Prophets may predict future events*

Agabus demonstrated this when he predicted the coming famine. The Jewish historian Josephus confirmed this famine. This was not the only time that Agabus ministered predictively, but it was significant.[51]

2. Prophets may confirm direction

Although Paul would not be deterred from the direction he was going (and rightly so), Agabus merely confirmed to the believers present, what Paul already knew. He would be bound and taken captive, but coming from a man who had survived stonings, beatings, imprisonments, and more, what was new about this upcoming experience?[52]

3. Prophets may possess an extraordinary boldness

Historically prophets did not fare well as a result of their prophetic ministry. The very first prophet, Abel,[53] was killed by his own brother. That pattern has continued throughout history as numerous prophets have experienced death at the hands of their brethren. Knowing this has been their lot would imply a degree of

---

[51] Acts 11:28
[52] Acts 21:10-14
[53] Matthew 23:35

boldness to be willing to speak what may not be deemed popular. The current climate of political correctness that we live under at the present time would merely be fodder to the prophetic voice to speak loudly and forcefully against it.

Jeremiah instructed the prophets this way:

> "The prophet who has a dream, let him tell a dream; And he who has My word, let him speak My word faithfully. Jeremiah 23:28 (emphasis mine)

Modern day prophets can do no less than faithfully speak the word of the Lord.

4. *Prophets may uncover hidden things*

As "seers," prophets see! Profound, is it not? However, they often will see things that others would like to have hidden or had remained hidden. They are often like the maid going into the hotel room and stripping the sheets off the bed. These New Testament prophets will often unveil what activities, ambitions, motives, hidden sin, and much more, is underneath. Prophets are part of the system of checks and balances that the church needs to keep their focus on holiness and obedience. They may come off as "hard-nosed," but they often have to be. They must demonstrate a flinty-faced determination to speak the word of the Lord.

The loss of this seeing aspect in the body of Christ has resulted in unnecessary time delays in establishing the Kingdom of God upon the earth and the discipling of nations. Having depended on upon the arm of the flesh, much has gotten done, but how much more could have been accomplished had we utilized the seer capabilities available to the body of Christ?

5. *Prophets often experience labeling*

In the Old Testament, you will find numerous stories of prophets being referred to as "crazy," or worse. That has not changed to this day. People often have a picture in their mind of a wild-haired man dressed in animal skins, eating grasshoppers and shouting from the street corners. Although they may, that is not necessarily the case. Though few wish to be labeled, it is unfortunately prevalent; do not be surprised if you as a prophet experience it.

6. *Prophets may be called upon to do the bizarre*

Ezekiel had to eat dung,[54] and Isaiah had to walk around naked for a time[55]. Although I do not expect that to be the norm (it happened only once in history to my knowledge), it is fair to say that God will demand that prophets do things that may seem bizarre to some. It is with these "foolish acts" that God confounds the wise.[56]

7. *Prophets will decree the Word of the Lord*

Prophets are the mouthpiece of the Lord. They provide the clarion call to what God is saying and doing in the earth. Often they will have to live out what their message is (or will be) long before it is actually voiced. When they are able to align with the apostolic voice, it provides a dynamic duo that breaks things open in regions and territories. The apostolic needs the prophetic and the prophetic needs the apostolic.

---

[54] Ezekiel 4:12
[55] Isaiah 20:2-3
[56] 1 Corinthians 1:27

Evangelists

>...and He gave some...evangelists. Ephesians 4:11

Again, we see an office that has multiple realms of influence and authority. We do not see a lot of mention of the evangelist in the book of Acts, but what we do see is dramatic. We are more likely to see those who were not necessarily called as an evangelist, but who performed the role of one with tremendous results.

An evangelist is a proclaimer of good news. Jesus, in Luke 4:18 (quoting from Isaiah 61) announced what sounds like a good description of the work of an evangelist:

> [18]"The Spirit of the Lord is upon me, because he has anointed me to preach the gospel to the poor; he has sent me to heal the brokenhearted, to proclaim liberty to the captives, and the recovery of sight to the blind, to set at liberty those who are oppressed; [19]to proclaim the acceptable year of the Lord" Luke 4:18-19

Philip the Evangelist

In Acts 21:8 we read of Philip, the evangelist.

> On the next *day,* we who were Paul's companions departed and came to Caesarea, and entered the house of Philip the evangelist, who was *one* of the seven and stayed with him.

Not only did he operate in the Ascension Gift of an evangelist, but he was also one of the seven original deacons we read the story of earlier in the book of Acts. Acts 8 gives us some insights into his life and ministry:

> ⁴Therefore those who were scattered went everywhere <u>preaching the word</u>. ⁵Then Philip went down to the city of Samaria and preached Christ to them. ⁶And the multitudes with one accord heeded the things spoken by Philip, hearing and seeing the <u>miracles which he did</u>. ⁷For unclean spirits, crying with a loud voice, <u>came out of many who were possessed</u>; and many who were <u>paralyzed and lame were healed</u>. ⁸And there was great joy in that city. Acts 8:4-8 (emphasis mine)

Philip's ministry was noted for preaching the word, exorcising demons, and great healings. That is a New Testament testimony of what we should see today. Some who are called evangelists only speak of salvation with the focus on conversions, but Philip went a couple of steps farther—ministering deliverance AND ministering healing and miracles as well as preaching the Word.

Luke goes on to describe his ministry and its impact:

> ¹²But when they believed Philip as he preached the things concerning the kingdom of God and the name of Jesus Christ, both men and women were baptized. ¹³Then Simon himself also believed; and when he was baptized, he continued with Philip, and was amazed, seeing the miracles and signs which were done. Acts 8:12-13

Philip's message was the Kingdom of God, and the result was many conversions in Samaria—an area unreached with the Gospel since Jesus brought life to the woman at the well. In Acts 8:26-40 we have the story of Philip's supernatural ministry to the Ethiopian steward or "official"[57] (some translations call him a eunuch, but a eunuch would not have been able to go to Jerusalem and worship at the Temple according to Jewish custom). One translation simply refers to him as a "believer." In any case, once he encounters Philip who was following an angel's instruction, he responds to Philip's explanation of the Gospel and is baptized immediately in water by Philip who is then

---

[57] Williams New Testament

supernaturally translated. Philip finds himself in Azotus, quite a distance away (Acts 8:26-40).

Paul notes Philip's ministry when they come together as recorded here:

> [8] On the next *day,* we who were Paul's companions departed and came to Caesarea, and entered the house of Philip the evangelist, who was *one* of the seven and stayed with him. Now this man had four virgin daughters who prophesied. Acts 21:8-9

Apparently, Philip had not neglected his family for the sake of his ministry, as his four daughters were following God as well. This is an example many in the ministry today would do well to follow. In recent years we have seen many who "for the sake of the ministry" neglected their families. Might some have been tested by their successful revival meetings while failing to take care of their family?

I recall hearing of a minister who was intending to divorce his wife because she did not seem to be as spiritual as he thought himself to be. Holy Spirit spoke to him and said, "Why should I let you take care of My bride when you will not take care of your own?"

When our ministry takes precedence over our families, some course correction is needed. All success is not from God. Our enemy would love to derail our lives, ministries, and influence by success. We must learn that we always have a responsibility to maintain our God-given relationships with our spouse and children and never forsake them even for the sake of the ministry. What may be called the "sake of the ministry," might, in fact, be "the sake of our pride." Know the difference and do the right thing! It has not been too long ago that the world witnessed the marriage breakup of the very famous evangelist, Benny Hinn. Thankfully, both sought help, and God restored their marriage, resulting in their ultimate remarriage in 2013 after having been divorced for three years.

Paul & Barnabas Evangelizing

Paul and Barnabas, though not titled evangelists, were known for their evangelism efforts out of which several churches were started in Asia Minor and other locales.

> [35]Paul and Barnabas also remained in Antioch, teaching and preaching the word of the Lord, with many others also. [36]Then after some days, Paul said to Barnabas, "Let us now go back and visit our brethren

in every city where we have preached the word of the Lord and see how they are doing." Acts 15:35-36

Coupled with Paul and Barnabas' evangelistic efforts was a desire to check on the new converts. This may have come forth as a result of their apostolic or prophetic or teaching callings, but in any case, it is a necessary component to evangelism. To evangelize and make no provision for the new converts' subsequent discipleship is to do them a disservice. You are birthing bastard children—orphans who have no spiritual fathers or mothers. We live in a culture where it is increasingly fashionable to have a baby but let someone else raise it. This mindset has infiltrated the church. If we, as the church, will repent of this grave sin, we will see God restore us and bring about the needed correction. Deuteronomy 23:2 warns us of the dire consequences of illegitimacy:

> "One of illegitimate birth shall not enter the assembly of the LORD; even to the tenth generation none of his *descendants* shall enter the assembly of the LORD. Deuteronomy 23:2

Ironically, in our efforts to bring people into the Kingdom, if we do so incorrectly, we are setting them up for failure in their walk with God. We must take responsibility for the upbringing of those we birth into the Kingdom.

When a new believer comes to faith in Jesus, they are in a very vulnerable state, just as a newborn infant would be. If you, in the natural, were to treat your newborn the way some evangelists treat their converts, it would be no surprise that Social Services would arrive on your doorstep and have something to say.

Recently I have seen someone functioning as a pastor who is really an evangelist. However, they have made no real provision for discipling the hundreds of converts they regularly boast about that result from their regular evangelistic outreaches. Out of all the so-called converts, they have no more than one or two who are plugged into their church—and that is a generous assessment. They need to stop what they are doing, establish a quality program of discipleship, and take further responsibility for their converts. It is not enough to merely get them saved! Jesus gave explicit instructions not only to go, but also to make disciples, baptizing them, and teach them.

> [19]Go therefore and make disciples of all the nations, baptizing them in the name of the Father and of the Son and of the Holy Spirit, [20]teaching them to observe all things that I have commanded you; and lo, I am

with you always, *even* to the end of the age." Amen. Matthew 28:19-20

Once they have the strategies in place for discipleship, then they can resume their evangelistic outreach efforts. To birth a baby and then abandon that child would be criminal in the natural world we live in. It is just as much a criminal, irresponsible behavior in the body of Christ. Plenty of suitable discipleship material exists, and if you do not find something you want to use, then at least pair up with someone who is anointed for the task, just as Peter and John did when Philip had evangelized in Samaria.

In the 1 Corinthians 12:28 passage, the term "evangelist" is not used. However, Paul lists two appointments: (workers of) miracles and gifts of healings. These two appointments are the earmarks of an evangelist, so likely they describe the evangelist's work on a local level. Again, the body of Christ has suffered because of the lack of recognition of these wonderful appointments in the body of Christ. Though we might "ooh and aah!" over the miracles, we hear about that should be more commonplace than they are and we will celebrate the "big name" evangelists, we often neglect that working on a local level. Again, we are living out a principle of honor:

What you honor you have the benefit of

and

What you do not honor you do not have the benefit of.

Paul tells us that the body grows and is "fitly supplied" by what each part contributes to the whole (see Ephesian 4:16).

We have as modern day examples of the evangelists' ministry that of Reinhard Bonnke and his associate evangelist Daniel Kolenda. We also have Tommy and Elizabeth O'Dell (Tommy is the grandson of the late evangelist T.L. Osborn), as well as many others who are used to draw many to faith in Jesus and who do not shy away from the supernatural. As more and more of these God-ordained evangelists come forth, may we experience a massive sweeping of men, women, and children into the Kingdom of God. Then, let us step in and raise them up to become mighty sons and daughters of the Most High!

Timothy and the Work of an Evangelist

Though we find no mention of Timothy, the protégé of Paul, being referred to as an evangelist, we do find the third use of the term evangelist referring *to* Timothy in 2 Timothy 4:5:

But you be watchful in all things, endure afflictions, do the work of an evangelist, fulfill your ministry.

Since the term "evangelist" (a preacher of the Gospel)[58] comes from the word "*evangelizo*[59]" meaning "to announce good news," every believer shares the instruction to do the work of an evangelist, that is to preach and share the good news. Paul knew that his ministry was winding down, yet he was still invested in his son in the faith, Timothy, charging him to remember always to be demonstrating Jesus.

Evangelistic Manifestations

1. *Evangelists may demonstrate the power gifts*

In addition to operating in miracles and gifts of healings, evangelists may also operate in the gift of faith. These power manifestations (1 Corinthians 12:8-10) are part and parcel of their lifestyle and ministry. These

---

[58] Strong. From G2097; a *preacher* of the gospel: - evangelist.

[59] Strong. From G2095 and G32; to *announce good* news ("evangelize") especially the gospel: - declare, bring (declare, show) glad (good) tidings, preach (the gospel).

miraculous demonstrations through Philip's ministry had a profound effect on those who heard of them:

> And the multitudes with one accord heeded the things spoken by Philip, hearing and seeing the miracles which he did. Acts 8:6

These demonstrations caused them to open their minds to the message being preached. Meeting real needs in tangible ways opens hearts to the Gospel. The evangelistic gifting has this earmark of ministry that is a beautiful demonstration of the love God has for people.

1. *Evangelists may demonstrate exorcism on powerful levels*

The lack of intimidation by the devil enables evangelists to demonstrate the power of the resurrection through their ministry boldly. They have a keen understanding of what Jesus understood as written in Acts 10:38:

> ...how God anointed Jesus of Nazareth with the Holy Spirit and with power, who went about

doing good and healing all who were oppressed by the devil, for God was with Him.

The same power working through Jesus is the same power they understand to be working through them. In Acts 16 we find Paul demonstrating the work of an evangelist when he comes across the young girl with a python spirit. After a few days of her badgering him, Paul casts the spirit out of her, leaving her employers without a means of pimping her gift, as she no longer had any power to perform.[60] They, of course, become enraged, start a ruckus and blame Paul for it. This is not unlike the Jezebel spirit who does not mind being a problem but never wants to take responsibility for what ensues.

2. *Evangelists may experience supernatural translation*

Just as Philip experienced supernatural translation when he completed his mission to the Ethiopian steward[61] and found himself instantly in Azotus (approximately 20 miles), from which he ministered in all the cities until he came to Caesarea (approximately 45 miles from

---

[60] Acts 16:16-24
[61] See Acts 8:26-40

Azotus).[62] Though trans-relocations are not restricted to any believer, this is the only reference we have of this phenomenon occurring in the New Testament after the ascension of Jesus.

3. *Evangelists may demonstrate an uncanny level of boldness*

Evangelists, by the nature of their ministry, need to be bold. They need to be willing to confront darkness and those living in darkness. In Acts 8, the death of Stephen is described. Immediately following that we find that Philip went from Jerusalem to Samaria and preached Christ to them[63] The backdrop for Philip's actions involved the newly unleashed persecution of the Christians[64] by the Jews as demonstrated in the stoning of Philip. It is one thing to preach when everything is going well, but quite another to do so when your life may hang in the balance.

---

[62] Acts 8:40
[63] Acts 8:5
[64] Acts 8:1-5

4. *Evangelists are likely to operate in the word of knowledge and discerning of spirits*

These operations would be necessary as means of ministering healing and miracles. Paul demonstrated this, as mentioned before in Acts 16.

Teaching Pastors

An Overview

Pastors & Teachers

In this section, we will be discussing some ideas that may fall outside of our personal belief paradigms. As we have a tendency to insert our beliefs and experiences into the passages we read (we often do this about our eschatology), let us take a step back and consider what the Word of God says, regardless of what our experience or culture has dictated to us. Is it possible that we have been doing things wrong? I challenge you to admit to this and say, "Yes." Have we been sincere in what we have been doing? Undoubtedly the answer would again be "yes." However, it is possible to be both sincere and wrong at the same time. History demonstrates this over and over. Hitler was sincere. He was also wrong. Jim Jones was sincere, but he also was wrong. You get the point.

Since some debate exists over whether the gifts listed in Ephesians 4 comprise five distinct gifts or four (with pastor-teacher co-joined) as giftings to the body of Christ. We find no mention of the term "pastor" in Acts or the epistles as far as someone operating in that office. We do, however, find teachers mentioned in Acts 13:1:

> Now there were in Antioch, in the Church there—as Prophets and teachers—Barnabas, Symeon surnamed 'the black,' Lucius the Cyrenaean, Manaen (who was Herod the Tetrarch's foster-brother), and Saul.

Whether they were "pastor-teachers" (co-joined terms) or simply "teachers" (no co-joining of terms) we do not know. We do know that Barnabas and Saul were referred to in this passage as prophets and teachers, and were soon sent out on a missionary journey in an apostolic function. We have indications that both were teachers and useful in making disciples.

The context of the Ephesians 4 listing is not the local body of believers often referred to as the *ecclesia*, but rather the larger body of Christ[65]. Within, the concept of the pastor (which infers close proximity to the sheep) would not resolve with scripture when we look at 1 Corinthians 12:28 where God has placed in the local body (*ecclesia*) first apostles, secondarily prophets, thirdly teachers, and so on. I do not believe that Paul wrote accidentally.

---

[65] Ephesians 4:12 ...for the equipping of the saints for the work of ministry, for the edifying of the body of Christ.

He was very purposeful in his writings, whether a one-page letter to Philemon or a much more lengthy treatise such as to those Corinthians or Hebrews.

The word used for body in Ephesians 4:12 is *soma*,[66] meaning body as a sound whole. Paul carries this thought through verse 16 where he speaks of how every part of the body doing its part results in the body (the whole) increasing and growing in the love of God.

The body of Christ is described in these ways:

- **The Larger Body of Christ** (every believer around the world and in Heaven) made up of the local expressions, which is made up of the individual members;
- **The Local Body of Christ** (the local *ecclesia*) - a smaller unit of the body of Christ, made up of even smaller units (the individual members);
- **The Individual Believer** - is the body of Christ in an individual fashion, but as a member of the local body of Christ, they are also part of the universal body of Christ. (Study Romans 12, 1 Corinthians 12, Ephesians 4)

---

[66] Strong. G4839. *soma*

Only one person in the New Testament could we consider being "called" as a pastor. That would be Peter where we find Jesus telling him to feed His lambs, feed His ewes, feed His sheep (see John 21:16-17). Peter is never referred to as a pastor anywhere in the New Testament but rather is referred to as an apostle. He is noted to have been a preacher & teacher of the Word (Acts 4:18; 5:25, 28, 42). Teachers were mentioned as well (Acts 13:1, Acts 15:35; Acts 18:11; 1 Timothy 2:7, 2 Timothy 1:11).

Teaching Pastors or Pastor/Teachers

The late Greek scholar Kenneth Wuest had this to say about the Ephesians 4:11 passage:

> *The men to whom God has given special gifts for ministering in the Word as given in verse eleven are apostles, prophets, evangelists, and teaching pastors. The construction in the Greek does not allow us to speak of pastors and teachers as two individuals here. The two designations refer to a pastor who also has the gift of teaching. The two gifts go together in the divine economy, and it, therefore, follows that a God-called pastor is to exercise a didactic ministry. That is, his*

> *chief business will be to teach the Word of God. His ministry is a ministry of explaining in simple terms what the Word of God means.* [67]

Definition of Pastor

Pastor – Shepherd, a tender-feeder, to tend and feed

Jesus is referred to as the great shepherd of the sheep (Hebrews 13:20):

> For ye were as sheep going astray but are now returned unto the Shepherd and Bishop of your souls. 1 Peter 2:25

Paul, in his closing address to the elders, gathered at Meletus, said this:

> Therefore, take heed to yourselves and to all the flock, among which the Holy Spirit has made you overseers, to shepherd the church of God which He purchased with His own blood. Acts 20:28

---

[67] Golden Nuggets from the Greek New Testament (p.36) Kenneth S. Wuest, Wm. P. Eerdman's Publishing, Grand Rapids, MI ©1941

Paul referred to them as overseers, but not pastors.[68] These were the elders of the Ephesian churches gathered at Paul's request as he was going to Jerusalem, and ultimately to Rome. No one was ever designated pastor from what we can read. Among these elders, we know have apostles, prophets, and teachers, which are described in other places.

The analogy of a shepherd to sheep is a common analogy in our experience, but characteristics of a sheepfold have some limitations that are not necessarily apropos to a local body of believers charged with discipling nations.

Author Jim Wies discusses this quite well in "His Glorious House":

> *Am I saying that the church does not need pastors and pastoral leaders? On the contrary, the church needs pastoral ministry more than ever. But let's define Biblical pastoral ministry and we will discover a few things that will change our perspective of exactly what a pastor is. It is my strong opinion that an effective church needs a whole team of pastors to effectively "pastor" a church. If we look at the job description*

---

[68] Strong. G4166. *poimēn* - Of uncertain affinity; a *shepherd* (literally or figuratively): - shepherd, pastor.

found in Ezekiel 34:1-16 most present-day pastors cringe.

"And the word of the LORD came to me, saying, "Son of man, prophesy against the shepherds of Israel, prophesy and say to them, 'Thus says the Lord GOD to the shepherds: "Woe to the shepherds of Israel who feed themselves! Should not the shepherds feed the flocks? "You eat the fat and clothe yourselves with the wool; you slaughter the fatlings, but you do not feed the flock "The weak you have not strengthened, nor have you healed those who were sick, nor bound up the broken, nor brought back what was driven away, nor sought what was lost; but with force and cruelty you have ruled them" (Ezekiel 34:1-4).

For thus says the Lord GOD: "Indeed I will search for My sheep and seek them out. "As a shepherd seeks out his flock on the day he is among his scattered sheep, so will I seek out My sheep and deliver them from all the places where they were scattered on a cloudy and dark day." (Ezekiel 34:11,12).

"I will feed My flock, and I will make them lie down," says the Lord GOD. "I will seek what was lost and bring back what has driven away, bind up the broken and strengthen what was sick;" (Ezekiel 34:15,16).

We see here that the Lord rebuked the shepherds who failed to feed the flock, strengthen them, gather them, heal them, bind up the broken and protect them from

> *harm. It is the description of one who protects, corrects, guides and provides. In essence, this can be described as the "ministry of feeding and caring" as expressed in these tangible ways. A pastor will feed the people with knowledge and understanding from anointing to teach and impart Biblical truth. But he will also bear the people in his heart; will pray for healing when they are hurting and sick; will tend to their soul, and will round them up when they are drifting away. A pastor is the expression of the individual care that Jesus has for His flock.*[69]

He goes on to discuss how, using this understanding of the pastor, that one individual can only effectively "pastor" 50 to 80 people, which coincidentally, the average size of most churches in America.

> *...what we have is many churches built on pastoral foundations rather than apostolic/ prophetic ones, that grow to about 50 to 75 people and plateau. To do the job effectively, it takes a team. (Wies, 76)*

---

[69] His Glorious House by Jim Wies, Oracle Publishing Services ©2014 (p.75-76).

Definition of Teacher

Teacher – an instructor, master

Duty – to instruct in sound doctrine; to rightly divide the Word

Kenneth Wuest said this about teaching-pastors:

The two gifts go together in the divine economy, and it, therefore, follows that a God-called pastor is to exercise a didactic ministry. That is, his chief business will be to teach the Word of God. His ministry is a ministry of explaining in simple terms what the Word of God means. The word 'pastor' is a Greek word which means 'a shepherd.' The illustration is evident. The pastor is to bear the same relationship to the people to whom he ministers that a shepherd does to his flock of sheep.[70]

---

[70] Golden Nuggets from the Greek New Testament (p.36) Kenneth S. Wuest, Wm. P. Eerdman's Publishing, Grand Rapids, MI ©1941

What is the pattern?

1 Corinthians 12:28-30 speaks of the local body

> ²⁸And God has appointed these in the church: first apostles, second prophets, third teachers, after that miracles, then gifts of healings, helps, administrations, varieties of tongues. ²⁹Are all apostles? Are all prophets? Are all teachers? Are all workers of miracles? ³⁰Do all have gifts of healings? Do all speak with tongues? Do all interpret?

Where were these appointed?

…And God has appointed these in the church[71]

"church" - *ecclesia*[72] – assembly of called out ones, a local body of believers

That local body and its surrounding community are their spheres of influence. Once the working of miracles and gifts of healing have been released to bring in a harvest, the need exists

---

[71] 1 Corinthians 12:28

[72] Strong. G1577. *ecclesia* - Christian community of members on earth or saints in heaven or both): - assembly, church.

for the new converts to become disciples. That is where the teaching/pastor comes in. However, instead of working hand-in-hand, our pastor-centric model has focused the senior leadership of the church solely on the pastoral position. That shortchanges the church in its effectiveness. We need every part doing its part. Paul goes on to ask:

> [29] Are all apostles? *Are* all prophets? *Are* all teachers? *Are* all workers of miracles? [30] Do all have gifts of healings? Do all speak with tongues? Do all interpret?
> 1 Corinthians 12:29-30

The obvious answer is "no." They do not need to be, but we all need to be released to function where God has appointed us.

Teaching Pastor Manifestations

1. *Teaching Pastors will grow the believers into a dynamic force*

Because they are not encumbered with the management responsibilities inherent in running a church organization, these individuals can focus on teaching and grow the steady stream of converts being brought into the church by those functioning in the working of miracles and gifts of healings. Luke tells us that the early church grew daily. Growth was not only explosive (i.e., the Day of Pentecost), but also ongoing. The church grew from 120 believers in the upper room to now over 2 billion on the earth—and that number is steadily increasing!

2. *Teaching Pastors provide the nurturing necessary to help new believers acclimate to their new existence.*

Just as newborn babies are dependent upon adults to help them survive and learn to thrive in the new world to which they have come, so it is with new believers. They must learn how to relate to the world from a Kingdom mindset. That involves retraining and rethinking ways of doing things. Teaching pastors can help bring this about by providing the necessary hands-on care new believers often need until they can stand on their own.

3. *Teaching Pastors provide the bridge between newfound faith and mature faith*

As mentioned above, teaching pastors are instrumental in the ongoing growth of the new believer, but it does not stop at that point. They help the new believer learn how to identify with and work within the culture of the church, this assembly of called out ones that often resembles a menagerie of people from all walks of life, from the prim and proper to the biker types.

4. *Teaching Pastors provide counsel to the family*

As believers grow, they never stop having situations where they need counsel. Teaching pastors are uniquely equipped for this work. Often, they are strong in the mercy motivation and provide comfort, whereas the prophetic or apostolic mindset is entirely different. The church needs all the various types working together.

Comparing the Gifts

GIVER			
Holy Spirit	**Jesus**	**God**	**Holy Spirit**
charisma	*didomai*	*tithemi*	*phanerosis*
SCOPE			
The body of Christ-Individually	Body of Christ-Universally	Body of Christ-Locally *The Ecclesia*	Individual Believer
GIFT			
Prophecy	Apostles	Apostles	Word of Wisdom
Serving	Prophets	Prophets	Word of Knowledge
Teaching	Evangelists	Teachers	Faith
Exhorting	Teaching/Pastors	Miracles	Gifts of Healings
Giving		Gifts of Healings	Working of Miracles
Ruling		Helps	Prophecy
Mercy Show-er		Administration	Discerning of spirits
		Various Tongues	Various Tongues
		Interpretation of Tongues	Interpretation of Tongues

SECTION 5

Church Government

An Overview

Major Types

- Episcopal – Bishops, Priests/Ministers, Deacons (Top Down Style)
- Presbyterian – Representative Democracy, Congregation elects presbyters, elders, Board of Directors
- Congregational – Congregation votes on everything, Baptists (based on the "priesthood of believers")
- Consensus – Quaker/Friends, the universal agreement required before any action is taken

In this book, I will not be discussing the details of these various forms of government. However, I will provide a simple flowchart to give an overview of them and the most basic of details. Following the four mentioned above will be two different flow charts of the apostolic model as seen in the book of Acts (in particular).

Author Jim Wies, who embraces the five-fold view, pointed this out in his book, *His Glorious House*:

> *Much of the church structure of the 20th century is an old wineskin that cannot contain the wine that God is going to pour out for a final harvest at the end of the age. For instance, nowhere in the New Testament do we find a pastor being the sole minister of a local church. What we do see is churches led by apostles over teams of ministers; some of which were prophets, pastors, teachers, evangelists, administrators, many under the general "catch-all" grouping of "elders." The common government of the New Testament was a plurality of elders, made up of a diversity of offices and giftings who recognized within their midst headship, diversity of gifting, apostolic grace to lead, and prophetic grace to cast forth the vision.(Wies, 76)*[73]

He goes on to say,

---

[73] *His Glorious House* by Jim Wies, Oracle Publishing Services ©2014 p.74.

> *"But" you might ask, "what of the few very large churches that are led by pastors"? The very simple answer is that there are a number of churches built on the anointing and gifting of an apostle who is being called "pastor," or teaching ministries who are calling themselves "pastors," or prophets who are being called "pastors." Or evangelists who gather multitudes, who, while not pastoring them, yet are being called "pastors." (Wies, 77)*

Years ago, Holy Spirit spoke to me, saying that my impact as a senior leader in a church would be affected by whether I chose to be biblically-based in my approach and implementation, or culturally-based. I chose to be biblically-based, and it took retraining my own mindsets as well as the mindsets of those assigned to work with me. In some ways, we were successful, and in others, we still had a learning curve. People always come to a church with certain expectations, presuppositions, and beliefs of how they think things should be done. If they grew up in a particular denomination, they would often carry those mindsets into the new setting. Sometimes it puts undue pressure on the leadership of the new church too and can often break their focus if those coming in have expectations that things ought to be done a certain way. It often takes great determination on the part of the leadership to stay the course, and it takes a quality decision on the part of the body to stay the course with their leadership even through the occasional storms that arise. Paul warned us that storms would arise if only to measure where our commitment level was to that body.[74]

---

[74] 1 Corinthians 11:18-19

Episcopal Form of Government

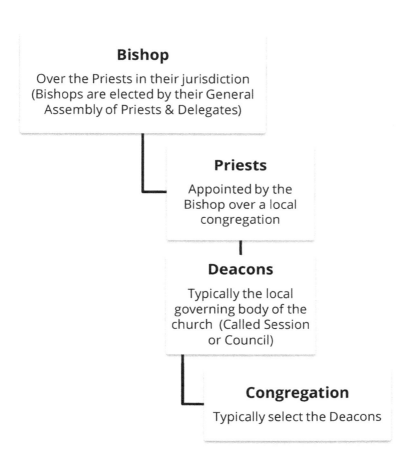

Presbyterian Form of Government

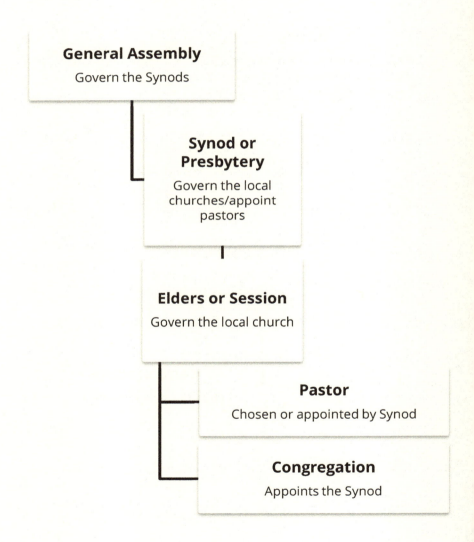

Congregational Form of Government

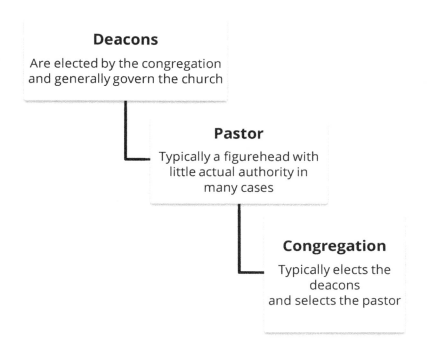

Consensus Form of Government

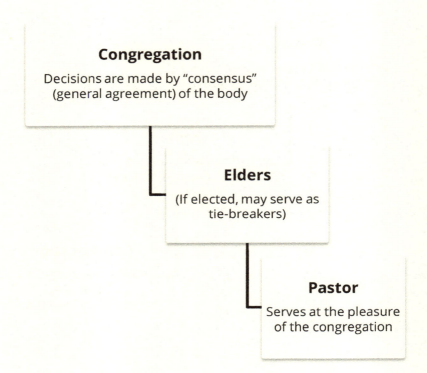

New Testament Church Government

As the church of Jesus Christ, our pattern for New Testament Church Government is found in no other place than the New Testament. The book of Acts modeled church government for us as they experienced it, while the epistles simply gave further directives or clarification to what we can see in the book of Acts. The late Dr. C. Peter Wagner, in discussing the re-emergence of the apostolic and prophetic in church government, had this to say,

> *Ephesians 2:20 tells us that the foundation of the church is apostles and prophets. This reflects not just a historical phenomenon which ceased shortly after Jesus departed and His apostles died, but it is a reality in the church today. The Bible says, "And God has appointed these in the church: first apostles, second prophets, third teachers" (1 Cor. 12:28). We are now dealing with a paradigm shift reflected in our understanding of Ephesians 4:11, which tells us that Jesus at His ascension "gave some to be apostles, some prophets, some evangelists, and some pastors and teachers." We used to be comfortable with pastors, teachers, and evangelists as governing church offices,*

but somehow we skipped over the offices of apostle and prophet. We are now correcting this, and the Holy Spirit is showing us how we reestablish the full biblical church government.[75]

New Testament leadership was vested in the apostles, prophets, and teachers (i.e., elders) from what we can see. Three categories of people are shown: apostles, elders, and brethren. The elders were apparently comprised of the apostles, prophets, and teachers (and possibly evangelists) among them, with one of the apostles taking on the role of Chief Apostle. James is a good example of one operating as the Chief Apostle. *(This was discussed in Section 4.)*

When it came to disciplinary matters, the apostles and elders, basically a local church council, discussed the issue and came up with a consensus. This consensus we are familiar with when reading Acts 15:25, 28 where it, "seemed good to the Holy Spirit and to us."

A particular understanding seemed to exist among the early church that God would help in the administration of correction

---

[75] Wagner, C. Peter (2015-10-20). Breaking Spiritual Strongholds in Your City (Kindle Locations 103-109). Destiny Image, Inc.. Kindle Edition.

when it was needed, whether it was among the brethren (congregation) or among the leadership. Jesus gave directives on dealing with conflict in Matthew 18:15-17. The apostle Paul also exercised his voice in addressing sin in the church as he did with the Corinthian church and the man sleeping with his father's wife, and we certainly know Peter did in dealing with Ananias and Sapphira.

In no way am I excusing leaders who get out of line morally or otherwise; however, we may have contributed to the issue by our form of government. For instance, if the pastoral role was never intended to be the senior leadership position in a church and yet someone with a pastoral/teaching anointing is put in that position, we have done them a disservice. It is likely that their motivational gift mix is not of the right makeup to be able to handle conflict, nor address sin in the church. The apostolic gift mix is likely to be much better geared to deal with those scenarios. The pastoral person is likely to be mercy motivated and dealing with conflict usually involves a prophetic perceiver gift, or a ruler or teacher gift mix.

When someone who dislikes conflict is required to confront a negative situation, they are put in an awkward position. They need to be able to access an apostolic gift mix to deal successfully with the issue.

Further, when the only means a church has of dealing with conflict is via a church board of deacons, we are asking them to do something for which they are ill-equipped. Even if they are deacons (men or women) who have met the scriptural qualifications of being of good report, and full of the Holy Spirit, and full of wisdom, these qualifications make no provision for having the leadership strength to confront a negative situation and calling for it to stop.

Because we have lost the mechanism (via following a real New Testament model of government), we have also lost the ability to deal efficiently with sin situations in the local church. Since we have no mechanism, we cannot adequately deal with sin in the church, and therefore sin is given license to run rampant. Many of the questions we see now confronting the church are allowed because they were not cut off in their infancy before they were allowed to take root and grow into a forest of problems.

Holy Spirit provided the mechanism for church government, he provided the mandate (Matthew 28:18 "...go...make disciples."), and He provided the means via the empowering of His Spirit so that we could boldly proclaim the Gospel to the ends of the earth.

To adapt to the New Testament paradigm will require some things. Again, Jim Wies summarizes it well:

For the typical local church, that means several things regarding the ministry of the pastor. It means a willingness to recognize and make a place for a new wineskin of leadership and ministry. In many cases, it will take a whole new structuring of the government of the church making room for apostolic and prophetic foundation layers to work. (Wies, 77)

New Testament Pattern of Government

Local Apostle

Serves with the Elders but is the person ultimately responsible

Elders/Bishops

Elders serve with the Local Apostle to give oversight (Could include: Prophets, Teachers, Miracles, Gifts of Healings, Helps, Administrations, Tongues & Interpretation)

Body of Believers

Do the work of the ministry in cooperation with leadership

Deacons

Serve the body in natural matters

New Testament Pattern of Government Hierarchy

Upper Level Apostolic Team
Paul always deferred to the Jerusalem church

Regional Apostolic Team
Timothy was responsible
to defer to Paul

Local Apostle & Elders
Responsible to the
Regional Authorities

Congregation
Do the work of the ministry
& submit to local leadership

Spiritual Territories

An area that has not been directly addressed concerns the territories in the realm of the spirit that are impacted by these offices (or not impacted because of the lack of these offices being in place) in a city, state, or region. The late Dr. C. Peter Wagner, George Otis, Jr., and Ed Silvoso are three men at who has been at the forefront of understanding the apostolic, prophetic and other ministry gifts and their impact in the realm of the spirit. I will not be discussing these issues in any depth here but will say that regardless of how we govern our churches in the natural if we do not first govern them in the realm of the spirit, it will not make a lot of difference what we do. However, if we learn to govern by the spirit in the spirit, we will be able to accomplish much more.

The apostles and prophets need to help lead the charge in establishing and maintaining spiritual domination in their respective areas of responsibility. We must first govern in the spirit before we can ever govern in the natural arena. Dr. Wagner's book *Breaking Spiritual Strongholds in Your City* will give some useful insights as well as practical advice on this aspect of the apostolic and prophetic roles in establishing the Kingdom of God upon the earth in its fullness.

Each of the ministry gifts and appointments plays a vital role in fully establishing the domain of Jesus Christ as King of kings and Lord of lords in the earth. As we gain understanding, we will increase in impact, and powers of darkness will be routed, and Jesus will be glorified.

Elders

An Overview

Groups Within the New Testament Church

Acts 15:2 ...the apostles and elders (also v. 4, 6)

Acts 15:22 ...the apostles and elders with the whole church

Acts 15:23 ...the apostles and elders and brethren

Elders in the Modern Church

Certain groups and denominations recognize elders as a ruling body within the local church (i.e., Presbyterians, some Pentecostal groups). However, it has by no means become standardized. The International Church of the Foursquare Gospel utilizes a church "council." According to their website, the term "church council" is the functional equivalent of the board of directors, the board of trustees, the board of elders, etc.,[76] with the stipulation that this council not be comprised of other ministers. Their Handbook for Churches[77] outlines provision for Elders and Deacons as well. In the last few years, they have been revising their structure and allowing for the existence of non-chartered churches in what had been a denominational structure. This particular "reimagining" (as they call it) will gear them for greater Kingdom impact in the future.

No evidence exists in the New Testament that any elder was neither an Ascension Gift nor an Appointment to the local church – they all had ministry gifts of some sort.

Elders are not replacements for deacons. The two separate groupings had different functions: elders dealt with predominantly spiritual issues, and deacons handled practical issues, dealing with widows and orphans, etc. Some church groups have only Deacon Boards as the governing body for a local church. Typically, they are not comprised of men or women with an Ascension Gifting or Placement Gifting in the body of Christ, therefore—though they may have performed admirably—they are not qualified according to New Testament standards.

---

[76] www.foursquare.org
[77] http://www.foursquare.org/handbook/english.pdf (Section 16.1, 2) (2013)

Elders in the Modern Church

The elders, with the local apostle, are the decision-making body within the local church. The New Testament pattern of church government is not congregational; instead it is elder-led with a plurality of elders. In the absence of established elders in a local body, those with regional oversight were the decision makers (Timothy was to ordain elders in every church as was Titus). These churches already existed but did not have mature leadership in place. The direction for any church should be first the spiritual, then the natural realm; the spiritual always staying grounded to perform with honor, but not looking first to the natural arena to make determinations for direction.

The responsibility of Elders in the Local Church

- Anoint with oil and pray for the sick (when called upon) (James 5:14)
- Feed the flock (Acts 20:28; 1 Peter 5:2)
- Serve willingly (1 Peter 5:2)
- Take oversight (Acts 20:28)
- Be examples (1 Peter 5:3)
- Not lord over the flock (1 Peter 5:3)

> ¹The elders who are among you I exhort, I who am a fellow elder and a witness of the sufferings of Christ, and also a partaker of the glory that will be revealed: ²Shepherd the flock of God which is among you, serving as overseers, not by compulsion but willingly, not for dishonest gain but eagerly; ³nor as being lords over those entrusted to you, but being examples to the flock; ⁴and when the Chief Shepherd appears, you will receive the crown of glory that does not fade away. 1 Peter 5:1-4

Paul's Address to the Ephesian Elders

Just before Paul's departure for Jerusalem and then to Rome, upon landing at Miletus, he called for the elders of the Ephesian churches that were nearby. This is part of his address to them:

> ²⁸For I have not shunned to declare to you the whole counsel of God. ²⁸Therefore take heed to yourselves and to all the flock, among which the Holy Spirit has made you overseers, to shepherd the church of God which He purchased with His own blood. ²⁹For I know this, that after my departure savage wolves will come in among you, not sparing the flock. ³⁰Also from among yourselves men will rise up, speaking perverse

things, to draw away the disciples after themselves.
Acts 20:28-31

His concern for the churches had a pastoral element to it, but he never let that element overtake the overall responsibility to guard the church against those who would destroy it.

Why is this important?

- The measure of grace each office has is different;
- A more significant measure of grace rests upon the apostolic than the pastor-teacher due to the degree of responsibility. They do more. Therefore they need more grace for the task;
- A mercy oriented anointing cannot carry you through the tough places as easily;
- A mercy-oriented anointing will tolerate the unnecessary in your life and in the church;
- *A mercy-oriented anointing will not deal with the tough issues!*
- The apostolic, at every level, is a governing office;
- It does not tolerate that which will endanger the movement;
- It is willing to confront and conquer;

- It is more of a warring office (It is a Jehu – *take out the Jezebel* – anointing);
- It carries a different level of strength – particularly in spiritual warfare;
- The apostolic will bring a greater 'fear of the Lord';
- The pastoral (pastor-teacher) is a nurturing office – not an ordering office;
- The pastoral (pastor-teacher) is a mothering office vs. the fathering nature of the apostolic.

In the American church:

Some of the characteristics we currently see in American church:

- Little (if any) fear of the Lord in the church;
- Sin is not confronted in the church;
- Sin is tolerated, and if it is tolerated, it is condoned;
- You will tolerate what you are not willing to confront;
- What you will tolerate you will never change;
- What you never change will eventually change you;
- Few signs & wonders;
- Little evangelistic emphasis;
- Minimal "fathering" is occurring;

- Church duplication is almost non-existent;
- Deliverance is unheard of in the church.

Problems with the Wrong Setup

- No fear of God among the people;
- Do not deal with sin sufficiently;
- The support structure is not in place;
- Pastoral makeup is not sufficient for dealing with tough situations.

Bishops/Overseers

An Overview

Bishop - an overseer; a Christian in general charge of a church[78].

According to the late Bible Translator, James Murdock, D. Min. the only place the term for bishop occurred in the entire New Testament was in Acts 20:28:

> Therefore, take heed to yourselves and to all the flock, among which the Holy Spirit has made you overseers [bishops], to shepherd the church of God which He purchased with His own blood. (NKJV)

The New King James Version translates it as an overseer who may be in better keeping with the Aramaic root word involved. The Greek word is *episkopos* from which we get our word Episcopal. Although the New King James translates it usually as bishop, other translations use the term elder. The Greek *episkopos* is from root words meaning to take the oversight of.

---

[78] Strong. G1985. *episkopos*

This would appear to be in keeping with the 1 Corinthians 12:28 local apostle.

Our modern church culture seems to have misunderstood and abused the term bishop to the point that it usually has no direct relationship to a local church, but rather over a group of churches. When someone calls themselves a bishop, but he or she do not oversee anything, it is a misuse of the term. Early church writings indicate it would be more akin to the position we now often refer to as Senior Pastor; one who oversees the functions within that church body. They are the "Chief Elder" among a group of elders (a presbytery) that guide the ministry of the local church. We are currently seeing a more proper functioning of this when we see a multi-site church where one main church has developed daughter churches, each with its own unique personality, but still in alignment and relationship to the mothering church. Churches should almost always grow as a result of multiplication rather than division.

Early Church Father Ignatius often refers in his letter to the Ephesians concerning Onesimus as the Bishop overseeing the church at Ephesus. He praises the integrity and work of this man multiple times (See *The Epistle of Ignatius to the Ephesians*).[79]

Paul writes somewhat extensively on the characteristics of these individuals in the following passages:

> Paul and Timothy, bondservants of Jesus Christ, To all the saints in Christ Jesus who are in Philippi, with the bishops [elders] and deacons. Philippians 1:1

In this passage, we see Paul recognizing these individuals. When we recall that these churches were not small in number like we tend to think (Jerusalem was likely several thousand strong), we need to understand that these elders likely held specializations. One might focus his ministry in one arena such as the widows, and another would focus on the orphans, and another on the young, and so on. Each of these elders would possibly be "bishops" in their own right; whereas Timothy may have been recognized as a Regional Apostle, a Presiding Bishop over the region.

Peter refers to Jesus being our Chief Shepherd and Chief Bishop:

---

[79] Kirby, Peter. "Historical Jesus Theories." *Early Christian Writings*. 2016. 8 May 2016 <http://www.earlychristianwritings.com/text/1clement-hoole.html>.

> For you were like sheep going astray, but have now returned to the Shepherd and Overseer [Curator] of your souls. 1 Peter 2:25

In Philippians, we find:

> Paul and Timothy, the servants of Jesus Christ, to all the saints in Christ Jesus which are at Philippi, with the bishops and deacons. Philippians 1:1

The word 'bishops' is plural here, but only one primary church existed. It is likely referring to elders by the structure of the wording of bishops and deacons when other places it is elders and deacons. Elders are overseers (Acts 20:17, 28, Phil 1:1). The example of the church at Jerusalem was that the Local Apostle was the chief among the elders (See Acts 15).

Guidelines for Bishops - Responsibility of the Elders

Paul, in his letter to Timothy, outlines some of the qualifications of an elder/bishop/overseer:

> This *is* a faithful saying: If a man desires the position of a bishop, he desires a good work. ² A bishop then must be blameless, the husband of one wife, temperate, sober-minded, of good behavior,

hospitable, able to teach; ³not given to wine, not violent, not greedy for money, but gentle, not quarrelsome, not covetous; ⁴one who rules his own house well, having *his* children in submission with all reverence ⁵(for if a man does not know how to rule his own house, how will he take care of the church of God?); ⁶not a novice, lest being puffed up with pride he fall into the *same* condemnation as the devil. ⁷Moreover he must have a good testimony among those who are outside, lest he fall into reproach and the snare of the devil. 1Timothy 3:1-7

He gives similar instructions to Titus:

⁵For this reason I left you in Crete, that you should set in order the things that are lacking, and appoint elders in every city as I commanded you—⁶if a man is blameless, the husband of one wife, having faithful children not accused of dissipation or insubordination. ⁷For a bishop must be blameless, as a steward of God, not self-willed, not quick-tempered, not given to wine, not violent, not greedy for money, ⁸but hospitable, a lover of what is good, sober-minded, just, holy, self-controlled, ⁹holding fast the faithful word as he has been taught, that he may be able, by

sound doctrine, both to exhort and convict those who contradict. Titus 1:5-9

Responsibility to the Elders

Paul continues in giving understanding concerning the elders:

Honor Them

> Let the elders who rule well be counted worthy of double honor, especially those who labor in the word and doctrine. [18]For the Scripture says, "YOU SHALL NOT MUZZLE AN OX WHILE IT TREADS OUT THE GRAIN," and, "THE LABORER IS WORTHY OF HIS WAGES."[80]

The above passage speaks as clearly to the falsehood that those in the ministry should be willing to work for free, or for pauper's wages. The "Vow of Poverty" is a concept borne of a monk's personal conviction centuries ago and is quite ingrained in the Catholic psyche. Regarding living their version of a monastic lifestyle, they and those who subsequently served with them vowed to forsake money and earning a living and live off the generosity of others and what they are able to produce

---

[80] 1 Timothy 5:17

themselves within their order to sustain them. Scripture does not teach this; instead, Paul is saying something quite the opposite.

The embracing of the lie that those in ministry should only be paid the bare minimum to survive has brought a curse on entire church communities, for they are dishonoring those who labor among them and have caused them to live in such conditions as to bring rebuke upon Christianity. Am I defending some who may have gone to what appears an extreme in their lifestyle—no? Rather, the pendulum has been too long swung on the side of poverty and embracing the old adage:

> *"Lord, we'll keep the preacher poor, you keep him humble."*

Do not Falsely Accuse Them

Another aspect of responsibility *to* the elders is outlined in 1 Timothy:

> [19]Do not receive an accusation against an elder except from two or three witnesses. [20]Those who are sinning rebuke in the presence of all, that the rest also may fear. 1 Timothy 5: 19

> "They are just in it for the money."

"They do not care about us."

"I believe he is having an affair."

This set of instructions has to do with dealing with accusations against an elder. Quite simply, unless you have two or three witnesses minimum, you do not have grounds for an accusation. Remember too that the one bringing the accusation does not necessarily count as a witness. Much caution has to be exerted here so as to be honorable in dealing with issues concerning elders. The same caution needs to be exercised in dealing with issues concerning those within the church. Let us merely follow biblical precedent.

Deacons

Congregational Selection

The only recorded instance of congregational input in a selection process in the entire New Testament in Acts 6 where deacons were selected. The purpose of this selection was to facilitate the distribution of food to the Hellenist widows. No other responsibilities were given, and no further authority was given from what we know from Acts. It is assumed that this was the selection of deacons (Acts 6:2) because of the phrase "serve tables" (*diakonos*). It was not used for the selection of any other persons. We have no record of it ever being done again. Also, we must recall that the Church at Jerusalem was likely several thousand in number, so the apostles did not hurriedly go through this process.

> ¹Now in those days, when the number of the disciples was multiplying, there arose a complaint against the Hebrews by the Hellenists, because their widows were neglected in the daily distribution. ²Then the twelve summoned the multitude of the disciples and said, "It

is not desirable that we should leave the word of God and serve tables. ³Therefore, brethren, seek out from among you seven men of good reputation, full of the Holy Spirit and wisdom, whom we may appoint over this business; ⁴but we will give ourselves continually to prayer and to the ministry of the word." ⁵And the saying pleased the whole multitude. And they chose Stephen, a man full of faith and the Holy Spirit, and Philip, Prochorus, Nicanor, Timon, Parmenas, and Nicolas, a proselyte from Antioch, ⁶whom they set before the apostles; and when they had prayed, they laid hands on them. ⁷Then the word of God spread, and the number of the disciples multiplied greatly in Jerusalem, and a great many of the priests were obedient to the faith. Acts 6:1-7

Deacons:

- Facilitated the ministry to the widows;
- Enabled the Apostles & Elders to devote themselves to the Word of God and prayer;
- They were not a governing body, but a service team; (deacons are "helpers")
- Did not in any way select pastors or others for positions;

- Was not enacted until the church at Jerusalem had grown quite large – in the tens of thousands;
- Were comprised of seven men who were (1) of good reputation; (2) full of the Holy Spirit; and (3) full of wisdom.

The deacons of the early church were never charged with general oversight of the local church, nor were they charged with general oversight of the senior leadership of the church, whether called a pastor, apostle, elder, or anything else. No precedent exists in the New Testament for this commonly adopted system.

Whom did they choose?

Stephen, a man full of faith and the Holy Spirit (see v.8), Philip (the evangelist), Prochorus, Nicanor, Timon, Parmenas, Nicolas (a proselyte from Antioch).

Acts 6:7 tells us what was the result of their selection

> Then the word of God spread, and the number of the disciples multiplied greatly in Jerusalem, and a great many of the priests were obedient to the faith.

Would we not like that to be the result of our selections of deacons and other leaders?

The word deacon is translated that way 5 times in the NT (also translated as minister or servant) (Philippians 1:1, 1 Timothy 3:8, 10, 12, 13). In Romans 16:1 we have a record of a female deacon—Phebe. We find in Philippians 1:1 that the church at Philippi had established deacons, so the precedent for deacons is shown, but their function was always in the realm of service under the senior leadership, not oversight of senior leadership.

Paul gave an extensive list of requirements for bishops and deacons in 1 Timothy 3:8-13:

> [8]Likewise deacons must be reverent, not double-tongued, not given to much wine, not greedy for money, [9]holding the mystery of the faith with a pure conscience. [10]But let these (bishops) also first be tested; then let them serve as deacons, being found blameless. [11]Likewise, their wives must be reverent, not slanderers, temperate, faithful in all things. [12]Let deacons be the husbands of one wife, ruling their children and their own houses well. [13]For those who have served well as deacons obtain for themselves a good standing and great boldness in the faith which is in Christ Jesus.

We will not discuss these requirements because they are somewhat straightforward. Paul did make one exciting recommendation for bishops to first serve as deacons (v.10). Since all the giftings (whether Ascension Gifts or Appointments) are about service, a good training ground was apparently available when serving as a deacon.

It is important to note also that in 1 Corinthians 12, the appointments were made by God himself - not by a committee, not by a congregation, not by a deacon or elder board, nor by any other entity.

> But now hath God set (appointed, ordained, placed) the members every one of them in the body, as it hath pleased him. 1 Corinthians 12:18

What are YOU called to do?

Are you called/appointed?

    Apostle?

    Prophet?

    Teacher?

    Miracle worker?

    Gifts of healings?

    Helps?

    Administrations?

    Varieties of tongues?

    Interpretation of tongues?

OR,

    Apostle?

    Prophet?

    Evangelist?

    Pastor-teacher or teaching pastor?

Once we are able to effectively determine our placement and the scope of our ministry (and if you cannot identify the placement, then first seek to identify the scope of your ministry), we will be better able to step into that place and accelerate the process of building the Kingdom of God. The Kingdom of God is not coming—it is already here. We must be about the Father's business of fully establishing it in the earth.

As you have read from my journey of the treasure hunt, I discovered things I only suspected, but never understood, and by no means do I pretend to understand them now. Yet if we will build upon each level of understanding, we will come to understand more thoroughly as time goes on. As more insight comes, we will be able to implement the new things Holy Spirit is showing us. The church is like a massive battleship that just does not turn on a dime. It takes several nautical miles to make a significant change in course. It will take the church a while to make the same course corrections.

For those of you who have functioned in the role of pastor, but never quite felt comfortable in those shoes. Hopefully, this book has answered a few questions. I appreciate and honor you for serving as a pastor to the body of Christ, but at the same time, we must accelerate the process of honoring the structure God set in place, which Paul described to us in 1 Corinthians 12:28-29.

First apostles, secondarily prophets, thirdly teachers, etc. If we do things God's way, then we can expect the results God had intended all along. We serve a victorious King in an ever-increasing Kingdom. The best days of the church are ahead of us, not behind. Let us go forward, full speed ahead!

Works Cited

Barnes, Albert. Isaiah 43 Barnes Notes. n.d. 30 August 2016 <http://biblehub.com/commentaries/barnes/isaiah/43.htm>.

Brenton, Sir Lancelot Charles Lee. Translation of the Greek Septuagint into English. Public Domain, n.d.

Brown, Francis, S.R. Driver, Charles A. Briggs, G.R.Driver, Wilhelm Gesenius, Wilhelm Gesenius, Eil Roediger and Edward Robinson. A Hebrew and English Lexicon of the Old Testament: With an Appendix Containing the Biblical Aramaic. Oxford: Clarendon, 1952.

Callaway, Ewen. "Fearful Memories Haunt Mouse Descendants." 1 December 2013. Nature News. 30 August 2016 <http://www.nature.com/news/fearful-memories-haunt-mouse-descendants-1.14272>.

Church of God in Christ, Inc. The Presiding Bishop. 16 May 2016. 10 October 2016 <http://www.cogic.org/cogic30/about-company/the-executive-branch/the-presiding-bishop/>.

Church, International Pentecostal Holiness. "Apostolic Postion Papers." 2016. www.iphc.org. 8 August 2016 <http://iphc.org/position-papers/ Apostolic Position Papers>.

Clarke, Adam. The Adam Clarke Commentary. 1832, Public Domain.

Crossway. ESV® Bible (The Holy Bible, English Standard Version®). Nashville: Good News Publishers, 2001.

Edition, Collins English Dictionary - Complete & Unabridged 10th. www.dictionary.com. 2 May 2016. 8 August 2016 <http://www.dictionary.com/browse/braggadocious>>.

—. www.dictionary.com. 2 May 2016. 8 August 2016 <http://www.dictionary.com/browse/braggadocious>>.

Fortune, Don & Katie. Discovering Your God-Given Gifts. Grand Rapids: Chosen Books, 2009.

Foundation, The Lockman. The Amplified Bible. Grand Rapids: Zondervan, 1958.

Fox, Stuart. Popular Science 7 January 2010.

God, Assemblies of. "Position Papers-Apostles & Prophets." 2016. www.ag.org. 8 August 2016

<http://ag.org/top/Beliefs/Position_Papers/pp_downloads/pp_4195_apostles_prophets.pdf>.

Gospel, International Church of the Foursquare. "Handbook." 2016. Foursquare.org. 8 August 2016 <http://www.foursquare.org/handbook/english.pdf>.

Hickey, Marilyn & Bowling, Sarah. Know Your Ministry. New Kensington: Whitaker House, 2012.

Kirby, Peter. Historical Jesus Theories Early Christian Writings. 2016. 8 August 2016 <http://www.earlychristianwritings.com/text/1clement-hoole.html>.

Merriam-Webster.com. http://www.merriam-webster.com/dictionary/protocol. n.d. 31 August 2016 <http://www.merriam-webster.com/dictionary/protocol>.

Moffat, James. James Moffat Translation of the New Testament. Chicago: The University of Chicago Press, 1926.

Murdock, James. James Murdock New Testament. 1851, Public Domain.

Phillips, J.B. Letters to Young Churches. Macmillan, 1947.

Strong, James. The New Strong's Expanded Exhaustive Concordance of the Bible. Nashville: Thomas-Nelson, 2010.

Thompson, Stephen. The Freedom Outpost. 2016. 8 August 2016 <https://youtu.be/WeSr_F7b7D8>.

Wagner, C. Peter. Breaking Spiritual Strongholds in Your City. Shippensburg: Destiny Image, Inc., 2015.

Weiss, Jim. His Glorious House. Maricopa: Oracle Publishing Service, 2014.

Wilson, Douglas. Heaven Misplaced: Christ's Kingdom on Earth. Kindle Edition: Canon Press, 2008.

Winter, Ralph D. and Koch, Bruce A. "Finishing the Task." 2016. www.frontierventures.org. 8 August 2016 <www.frontierventures.org>.

Wuest, Kenneth S. Golden Nuggets from the Greek New Testament. Grand Rapids: Eerdman's Publishing, 1941.

Made in the USA
Monee, IL
09 June 2021